Geography
Complete Revision and Practice

Denise Freeman, Nicola Twitchett

Published by BBC Active, an imprint of Educational Publishers LLP, part of the Pearson Education Group Edinburgh Gate, Harlow, Essex CN20 2JE, England

ISBN 978-1-4066-5441-7

Printed in China (CTPSC/03)

First published 2002

This edition 2010

10 9 8 7 6 5 4 3

Image acknowledgements

Cambridge Science Park: Photograph used by kind permission of Cambridge Science Park p101.

Denise Freeman: © Denise Freeman 2009 p50.

iStockphoto – all images used under licence from iStockphoto.com. Individual images © 2009 to photographer as follows: p20 Guenter Guni; p64 Salem.

London Aerial: p47 © London Aerial Photo Library.

EUMETSAT/Met Office: p8 and p57 (upper) © Copyright EUMETSAT/ Met Office 2009, data supplied by the Met Office; p57 (lower) © Crown Copyright 2009, the Met Office.

Ordnance Survey © Crown copyright 2009: p5, p130, p131.

Shutterstock: all images used under licence from Shutterstock.com. Individual images © 2009 to artist or photographer as follows: p6 robert paul van beets; p18 wanghanan; p45 Jiri Papousek; p51 Timothy Large; p60 (left) Albert Lozano; p63 (top) Alessio Ponti, (bottom left) EuToch, (bottom right) luchschen; p64 (right) thisorder; p91 witchcraft; p95 AridOcean; p112 Ewen Cameron; p116 (top right) Jennifer King, (top left) AridOcean.

specialist publishing services ltd – all images © specialist publishing services ltd 2009 except as indicated: p28; p41; p59 and p60 (right) (© Allison Walter); p75; p89 (© Barnaby Hutchins); p109 (top), (bottom) with thanks to Globe Theatre, London; p116 (© Paul Fennell); p119.

Contents

Exam board specification map   iv
Introduction   vi
Topic checker   x
Topic checker answers   xvi

Geographical skills

Using maps   2
Using images and analysing data   6
Using new technologies in geography   8

Natural hazards

Tectonic hazards   10
Earthquakes   14
Volcanoes   16
Case study – Sichuan earthquake   18
Case study – Mt Nyiragongo volcano   20
Tropical storms   22
Drought   24

Rocks and weathering

Rocks and weathering   26

Glaciation

Glaciation   28

Rivers

The river system   30
River processes   32
River landscapes and features   34
Flooding and hydrographs   36
Managing flooding   38

Coasts

Wave power   40
Coastal processes   42
Landforms created by erosion   44
Depositional landforms   46
Managing the coastline   48
Coastal case studies   50

Weather and climate

Weather and climate   52
UK weather   54
Depressions and anticyclones   56
Cold environments   58
Hot desert environments   62
Climate change   66
Managing the impacts of climate change   68

Ecosystems

Ecosystems 70
The rainforest ecosystem 72

Population

Population change 76
Managing population change 78
Migration 80

Urban settlement

Urban settlement 82
Challenges facing MEDC cities 84
Challenges facing LEDC cities 86
Sustainable urban living 88

The changing countryside

Urban sprawl 90
Changing farming in MEDCs 92
Changing farming in LEDCs 94

The global economy

Globalisation 96
The global economy 98
Changing industry in MEDCs 100
Changing industry in LEDCs 102

An unequal world

Measuring global differences in development 104
Trade, aid and development 106

Tourism

Tourism 108
Rural tourism in the UK 110
Tourism issues in LEDCs 112
Case study – Tourism in the Costa del Sol, Spain 114
Case study – Tourism in Kenya 116

Sustainable development

Sustainable development 118
Sustainable resource use 120
Resources and energy production 122
Managing water resources 124

Exam questions and model answers 126
Answers to practice questions 135
Web links *
Last-minute learner 145

* Only available in the CD-ROM version of the book.

Exam board specification map

Most exam specifications offer an element of choice as part of their GCSE course; there are often several optional topics included in the syllabus. It is likely that you or your teacher will have made decisions about which parts of the course to study. Therefore, you may not need to know everything listed below relating to the specification you have been following. You should check with your teacher what you need to know for your exam before you start revising.

You are also likely to have studied a range of case studies in class and these may not match the ones in this book. Check with your teacher which case studies you need to learn.

	page	AQA A	AQA B	Edexcel A	Edexcel B	OCR A	OCR B	WJEC A	WJEC B
Geographical skills									
Using maps 1	2	✔	✔	✔	✔	✔	✔	✔	✔
Using maps 2	4	✔	✔	✔	✔	✔	✔	✔	✔
Using images and analysing data	6	✔	✔	✔	✔	✔	✔	✔	✔
Using new technologies in geography	8	✔	✔	✔	✔	✔	✔	✔	✔
Natural hazards									
Tectonic hazards 1	10	✔	✔	✔	✔	✔	✔	✔	
Tectonic hazards 2	12	✔	✔	✔	✔	✔	✔	✔	
Earthquakes	14	✔	✔	✔	✔	✔	✔	✔	
Volcanoes	16	✔	✔	✔	✔	✔	✔	✔	
Case study – Sichuan earthquake	18	✔	✔	✔	✔	✔	✔	✔	
Case study – Mt Nyiragongo volcano	20	✔	✔	✔	✔	✔	✔	✔	
Tropical storms	22	✔	✔			✔*	✔		
Drought	24						✔	✔	
Rocks and weathering									
Rocks and weathering	26	✔	✔	✔	✔		✔	✔	✔
Glaciation									
Glaciation	28	✔			✔				
Rivers									
The river system	30	✔		✔	✔		✔	✔	✔
River processes	32	✔		✔	✔		✔	✔	✔
River landscapes and features	34	✔		✔	✔		✔	✔	✔
Flooding and hydrographs	36	✔		✔	✔		✔	✔	✔
Managing flooding	38	✔		✔	✔		✔	✔	✔
Coasts									
Wave power	40	✔	✔	✔	✔		✔	✔	✔
Coastal processes	42	✔	✔	✔	✔		✔	✔	✔
Landforms created by erosion	44	✔	✔	✔	✔		✔	✔	✔
Depositional landforms	46	✔	✔	✔	✔		✔	✔	✔
Managing the coastline	48	✔	✔	✔	✔		✔	✔	✔
Coastal case studies	50	✔	✔	✔	✔		✔	✔	✔
Weather and climate									
Weather and climate	52	✔						✔	✔
UK weather	54	✔						✔	✔
Depressions and anticyclones	56	✔						✔	✔
Cold environments 1	58	✔++	✔		✔	✔			
Cold environments 2	60	✔++	✔		✔	✔			

	Page								
Hot desert environments 1	62		✔		✔	✔			
Hot desert environments 2	64	✔**	✔		✔	✔			
Climate change	66	✔	✔	✔	✔	✔	✔	✔	✔
Managing the impact of climate change	68	✔	✔	✔	✔	✔	✔	✔	✔
Ecosystems									
Ecosystems	70	✔	✔		✔			✔	✔
The rainforest ecosystem 1	72	✔	✔	✔	✔			✔	✔
The rainforest ecosystem 2	74	✔	✔	✔	✔			✔	✔
Population									
Population change	76	✔		✔	✔	✔	✔	✔	
Managing population change	78	✔		✔	✔	✔	✔	✔	
Migration	80	✔		✔	✔	✔	✔	✔	
Urban settlement									
Urban settlement	82	✔	✔	✔	✔	✔	✔		✔
Challenges facing MEDC cities	84	✔	✔	✔	✔	✔	✔		✔
Challenges facing LEDC cities	86	✔	✔	✔	✔		✔	✔	✔
Sustainable urban living	88	✔	✔		✔	✔	✔		✔
The changing countryside									
Urban sprawl	90	✔		✔	✔			✔	✔
Changing farming in MEDCs	92	✔		✔	✔+				
Changing farming in LEDCs	94	✔**			✔+				
The global economy									
Globalisation	96	✔	✔	✔	✔	✔	✔	✔	✔
The global economy	98	✔	✔	✔	✔	✔	✔	✔	✔
Changing industry in MEDCs	100	✔	✔	✔	✔		✔	✔	✔
Changing industry in LEDCs	102		✔	✔	✔		✔	✔	✔
An unequal world									
Measuring global differences in development	104	✔	✔		✔	✔	✔	✔	✔
Trade, aid and development	106	✔	✔		✔	✔	✔	✔	✔
Tourism									
Tourism	108	✔	✔	✔				✔	
Rural tourism in the UK	110	✔	✔	✔	✔^			✔	✔^
Tourism issues in LEDCs	112	✔	✔	✔				✔	
Case study – Tourism in the Costa del Sol, Spain	114	✔	✔	✔				✔	
Case study – Tourism in Kenya	116	✔	✔	✔				✔	
Sustainable development									
Sustainable development	118	✔	✔	✔	✔	✔	✔	✔	✔
Sustainable resource use	120	✔		✔	✔	✔		✔	
Resources and energy production	122	✔		✔	✔			✔	
Managing water resources	124	✔		✔	✔				✔

* You should have studied a range of hazards: tropical storms may have been one of these hazards.

** The focus in this course is upon rural issues in tropical and subtropical areas. This is touched upon in this double-page spread.

^ Rural issues are studied on this course and so this page on UK National Parks may help your revision.

+ The changing countryside is studied on this course and so this page on farming may help your revision.

++ This course includes a unit of work called 'Ice on the land', these pages may help support your revision for this topic.

Introduction

How to use GCSE Bitesize Complete Revision and Practice

Begin with the CD-ROM. There are five easy steps to using the CD-ROM – and to creating your own personal revision programme. Follow these steps and you'll be fully prepared for the exam without wasting time on areas you already know.

Topic checker

Step 1: Check

The Topic checker will help you figure out what you know – and what you need to revise.

Revision planner

Step 2: Plan

When you know which topics you need to revise, enter them into the handy Revision planner. You'll get a daily reminder to make sure you're on track.

Step 3: Revise

From the Topic checker, you can go straight to the topic pages that contain all the facts you need to know.

- Give yourself the edge with the Web*Bite* buttons. These link directly to the relevant section on the BBC Bitesize Revision website.

- Audio*Bite* buttons let you listen to more about the topic to boost your knowledge even further. *

Step 4: Practise

Check your understanding by answering the Practice questions. Click on each question to see the correct answer.

Step 5: Exam

Are you ready for the exam? Exam*Bite* buttons take you to an exam question on the topics you've just revised. *

* Not all subjects contain these features, depending on their exam requirements.

Interactive book   You can choose to go through every topic from beginning to end by clicking on the Interactive book and selecting topics on the Contents page.

Exam questions   Find all of the exam questions in one place by clicking on the Exam questions tab.

Last-minute learner   The Last-minute learner gives you the most important facts in a few pages for that final revision session.

You can access the information on these pages at any time from the link on the Topic checker or by clicking on the Help button. You can also do the Tutorial which provides step-by-step instructions on how to use the CD-ROM and gives you an overview of all the features available. You can find the Tutorial on the Home page when you click on the Home button.

Other features include:

Click on the draw tool to annotate pages. N.B. Annotations cannot be saved.

Click on Page turn to stop the pages turning over like a book.

Click on the Single page icon to see a single page.

Click on this arrow to go back to the previous screen.

Contents   Click on Contents while in the Interactive book to see a contents list in a pop-up window.

Click on these arrows to go backward or forward one page at a time.

Click on this bar to switch the buttons to the opposite side of the screen.

Click on any section of the text on a topic page to zoom in for a closer look.

N.B. You may come across some exercises that you can't do on-screen, such as circling or underlining, in these cases you should use the printed book.

About this book

Use this book whenever you prefer to work away from your computer. It consists of two main parts:

1 A set of double-page spreads, covering the essential topics for revision from each of the curriculum areas. Each topic is organised in the following way:

- a summary of the main points and an introduction to the topic
- lettered section boxes cover the important areas within each topic
- key facts highlighting essential information in a section or providing tips on answering exam questions
- practice questions at the end of each topic – a range of questions to check your understanding.

2 A number of special sections to help you consolidate your revision and get a feel for how exam questions are structured and marked. These extra sections will help you to check your progress and be confident that you know your stuff. They include:

- exam-style questions and worked model answers and comments to help you get full marks
- Topic checker – quick questions covering all topic areas
- Last-minute learner – the most important facts in just a few pages.

Essential terms and concepts in GCSE Geography

The terms and ideas explained below are referred to throughout this book. They are very important in GCSE Geography and you need to make sure you learn them as part of your revision. Understanding and using the correct geographical terms in your exam can ensure that you gain valuable marks. Some exam boards expect you to know and understand specific terms and concepts. Check this with your teacher.

human geography the study of human activities, e.g. urban settlements

physical geography the study of natural processes, e.g. coastal erosion

Human and physical geography are very closely connected. For example, humans building sea defences can influence erosion along a stretch of coastline.

urban a built-up area, e.g. a town or city

rural an area of open land and generally low-population density, i.e. the countryside

LEDC Less Economically Developed Country. Some exam boards may use the term 'less developed country' or 'low income country' (LIC).

MEDC More Economically Developed Country. Some exam boards may use the term 'more developed country' or 'high income country' (HIC).

NIC Newly Industrialised Country

geographical patterns trends or patterns found across different parts of the world. Geographical patterns tell us what is happening in the world.

geographical processes these help to explain the world in which we live. For example, geographical processes can be used to explain how different landscapes are formed or why a city has grown in a particular way.

globalisation the process whereby people and places are becoming increasingly interconnected. As technology develops, the world seems to be getting smaller. People can now travel great distances at high speeds and the Internet allows us to make instant contact with distant people and places.

The process of globalisation has had an important effect on trade and production. Many individual countries and nations have become part of a single global economy. A financial or commercial setback in one country can have an impact on the whole world trade system.

sustainable development an important concept in geography. If something is sustainable, it can be kept going. Sustainable development meets people's present needs while conserving the natural environment for future generations.

About your exam

Get organised

You need to know when your exams are before you make your revision plan. Check the dates, times and locations of your exams with your teacher, tutor or school office.

On the day

Aim to arrive in plenty of time, with everything you need: several pens, pencils, a ruler and possibly mathematical instruments, a calculator or a language dictionary, depending on the exam subject.

On your way, or while you're waiting, read through your Last-minute learner.

In the exam room

When you are issued with your exam paper, you must not open it immediately. However, there are some details on the front cover that you can fill in before you start the exam itself (your name, centre number, etc.). If you're not sure where to write these details, ask one of the invigilators (teachers supervising the exam).

When it's time to begin writing, read each question carefully. Remember to keep an eye on the time.

Finally, don't panic! If you have followed your teacher's advice and the suggestions in this book, you will be well prepared for any question in your exam.

Topic checker

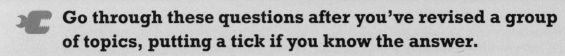

> Go through these questions after you've revised a group of topics, putting a tick if you know the answer.

> You can check your answers on pages xvi–xix.

>> Natural hazards

1	What causes the plates that make up the Earth's crust to move?	☐
2	Where are most of the world's volcanoes and earthquakes found?	☐
3	What happens at each type of plate boundary?	☐
4	What point on the Earth's surface is likely to suffer the greatest damage from an earthquake?	☐
5	Why do earthquakes sometimes occur in the same place as volcanoes?	☐
6	What is the difference between the primary and secondary effects of an earthquake?	☐
7	What can be done to restrict the damage caused by earthquakes?	☐
8	What causes a tropical storm?	☐
9	What is a drought?	☐
10	What are the impacts of drought in the Sahel?	☐

>> Rocks and weathering

11	How were igneous rocks formed?	☐
12	How were metamorphic rocks formed?	☐
13	What is the difference between weathering and erosion?	☐
14	What is the difference between physical and chemical weathering?	☐
15	Why are there so few streams in limestone areas?	☐

>> Glaciation

16	What is a corrie?	☐
17	What is the difference between abrasion and plucking?	☐
18	What different types of moraine are there?	☐
19	How can moraines provide evidence about the movement of a glacier?	☐
20	Describe two features of glacial deposition.	☐

>> Rivers

21	Which processes transfer water in the hydrological cycle?	☐
22	What is the discharge of a river?	☐
23	Name the four different methods by which material can be transported by a river?	☐
24	What is the difference between abrasion and attrition?	☐
25	Why do deltas sometimes form at the mouths of very large rivers?	☐
26	What factors influence the amount of discharge in a river?	☐
27	What two variables are shown on a hydrograph?	☐
28	What is lag time?	☐
29	What hard engineering methods can be used to manage flooding?	☐
30	What soft engineering methods can be used to manage flooding?	☐

>> Coasts

31	What is the difference between the swash and the backwash of a wave?	☐
32	How does the fetch of a wave affect its energy?	☐
33	What is the difference between constructive and destructive waves?	☐

Topic checker

34 What is the name given to the process of wave erosion resulting from changes in pressure caused when waves trap air in cracks in rocks and then retreat?

35 What is longshore drift?

36 How do stacks form?

37 What is the difference between 'hard' and 'soft' approaches to coastal management?

38 What are gabions and how do they help to reduce coastal erosion?

39 What are the advantages of building sea walls to protect areas of coastline?

40 What are the advantages of using 'beach nourishment' to protect a coastline?

>> Weather and climate

41 What is the difference between weather and climate?

42 What type of weather does a tropical continental air mass bring to Britain in summer?

43 Which air masses are most likely to bring snow and cold weather to Britain in winter?

44 How does the weather associated with a depression differ from the weather associated with an anticyclone?

45 Why do anticyclonic weather conditions often lead to poorer air quality and sometimes to the formation of smog over cities?

46 Where are cold environments (polar and tundra) located?

47 How do people use cold environments?

48 How is Antarctica protected against development?

49 Where are hot deserts found?

50 What is desertification?

51 What is global warming?

>> Ecosystems

52	What is the difference between the biotic and the abiotic parts of an ecosystem?	☐
53	What important role do decomposers play in ecosystems?	☐
54	Why is nutrient cycling so rapid in tropical rainforests?	☐
55	Why are large areas of rainforest being cleared in some areas?	☐
56	Why does deforestation result in a decline in the fertility of soils in tropical rainforests?	☐
57	How can rainforest areas be managed?	☐

>> Population

58	Why does the total population of a country grow during stage 2 of the Demographic Transition model?	☐
59	What factors cause birth rates to fall as a country develops?	☐
60	How is the population pyramid of a LEDC likely to be different to that of an MEDC?	☐
61	Why is the population of some MEDCs declining and what problems could result from this decline?	☐
62	How can 'push' and 'pull' factors be used to explain the causes of migration?	☐
63	What is a refugee?	☐

>> Urban settlement

64	In which parts of the world are cities growing most rapidly?	☐
65	What caused the inner-city area of many MEDC cities to decline during the 1960s and 1970s?	☐
66	How have some inner city areas been redeveloped and regenerated?	☐
67	What are 'squatter settlements'?	☐
68	How can 'self help' and 'site and service' schemes help to improve the quality of life in squatter settlements?	☐
69	What is an eco-town?	☐

Topic checker

| 70 | What is traffic calming and why may it be used? | ☐ |

>> The changing countryside

71	What is a green belt?	☐
72	What is counter-urbanisation?	☐
73	What are the impacts of counter-urbanisation?	☐
74	How is employment in farming changing in MEDCs?	☐
75	How are farmers trying to reduce the impact of farming on the environment?	☐
76	What is subsistence farming?	☐
77	What was the Green Revolution?	☐

>> The global economy

78	What is globalisation?	☐
79	What are TNCs?	☐
80	What are the four main sectors of industry?	☐
81	What is the typical employment structure for an MEDC?	☐
82	What is the typical employment structure for an LEDC?	☐
83	What is the knowledge-based economy?	☐
84	Name some recent NICs.	☐

>> An unequal world

| 85 | List three of the Millennium Development Goals. | ☐ |
| 86 | What is the 'balance of trade'? | ☐ |

87 What problems can LEDCs face if they rely on the export of a narrow range of primary products?

88 What are the three types of aid?

89 What are the disadvantages of large 'top-down' development projects?

90 What is grass roots development?

>> Tourism

91 Why has tourism become the fastest growing industry in the last fifty years?

92 What are the aims of a UK National Park?

93 What benefits can tourism bring for LEDCs?

94 What problems can tourism bring for areas in LEDCs?

95 What is sustainable tourism?

96 What are the advantages of eco-tourism?

>> Sustainable development

97 What is sustainable development?

98 What are the three Rs?

99 What is the difference between renewable and non-renewable sources of energy?

100 What are the disadvantages of coal as a source of energy?

101 What are the advantages of natural gas as a source of energy?

102 What are the causes of acid rain?

103 What are the limitations of wind power?

104 What is water stress?

105 How do the UK authorities manage water supplies?

Topic checker answers

>> Natural hazards

1	Convection currents
2	They are found on or near plate boundaries.
3	Constructive – plates move apart, magma rises and cools to form new land, volcanoes and earthquakes occur. Destructive – plates move towards each other, land destroyed, volcanoes and earthquakes occur. Conservative – plates slide past each other, earthquakes occur.
4	Close to the epicentre of an earthquake
5	Instability near plate boundaries and the huge pressure building up in subduction zones, where volcanoes form, can trigger earthquakes.
6	Primary – immediate impact, e.g. roads and buildings collapsing; secondary – result from damage caused by the initial tremors, e.g. fires caused by gas leaks from pipes fractured by the earthquake
7	Restrict building in areas prone to earthquakes; build earthquake-proof buildings that 'sway' rather than collapse; education and communication about what to do in an earthquake; earthquake monitoring and warning systems
8	A tropical storm (or tropical cycle or hurricane) is a low pressure system which develops over warm seas in the tropics.
9	A drought is when there is not enough rain over an extended period of time to support people or crops.
10	Mass migration of nomads and their livestock into the savannah. Some have moved to cities as refugees.

>> Rocks and weathering

11	When magma from inside the Earth cooled and solidified
12	When intense heat and pressure changed existing rocks, e.g. limestone into marble
13	Weathering is the breaking down of rocks, either at the surface of the Earth or underneath soil, without any movement of these rocks; erosion is the wearing away of rocks by water, ice or wind (i.e. involving movement).
14	Physical weathering usually results from large changes in temperature or pressure; chemical weathering occurs when chemicals dissolved in water attack and break down rock surfaces.
15	Limestone is a permeable rock (allowing water to pass through), so there are few streams on the surface.

>> Glaciation

16	Glaciers begin in hollows on the colder side of mountains. As the hollow becomes bigger, a corrie is formed.
17	Abrasion – rock fragments and ice act like rough sandpaper, wearing away rocks over which ice moves; plucking occurs when meltwater under a glacier freezes onto rock surfaces, pulling away large bits of rock when the glacier moves forward.
18	Medial, lateral and terminal
19	Different types of moraine are deposited at different places and at different stages in the movement of the glacier (e.g. terminal moraine will show the furthest point reached by the glacier).
20	Drumlins: mounds of boulder clay that have been shaped by the ice. Ice moves over them to form egg-shaped hills. Erractics: rocks transported many miles by the glacier and found in an area of different type

>> Rivers

21	Evaporation, transpiration, precipitation, infiltration, surface run-off (overland flow), throughflow, groundwater flow
22	The amount of water flowing in a river past a particular measuring point over a given period of time (measured in cumecs)
23	Traction, saltation, suspension and solution
24	Abrasion – material carried by rivers scrapes away the bed and banks; attrition – material carried by rivers breaks down into smaller fragments as it knocks into other material
25	Very large rivers carry vast amounts of sediment; as these rivers flow into the sea, they slow down, depositing material faster than it can be removed by the sea.
26	The weather, the geology of the area, land use around the river and whether the river has been engineered
27	Rainfall (measured in mm) and discharge (measured in cumecs)
28	Lag time is the difference (usually measured in hours) between peak rainfall and peak discharge.

29 Hard engineering methods include: building a dam (this allows people to control the flow of the river) or modifying the river channel (to make it wider, deeper or straighter).

30 Soft engineering methods include: afforestation (this helps intercept rainwater), allowing managed flooding or improved land use planning.

>> Coasts

31 Swash – movement of water up a beach; backwash – movement of water back down a beach

32 Waves with a larger fetch have more energy and stronger erosional power.

33 Constructive waves have a stronger swash and build up beaches; destructive waves have a stronger backwash and erode material from a beach.

34 Hydraulic action

35 The movement of material along a coastline in the direction of the prevailing wind

36 A stack forms when the roof of a natural arch in a headland collapses.

37 Hard approaches try to protect coastlines by deflecting or breaking up wave energy (working against natural processes); soft approaches work with natural processes to build up natural defences.

38 Gabions are wire baskets filled with rocks that try to reduce erosion by breaking down wave energy as waves bass between the rocks.

39 Sea walls protect the most vulnerable land uses by deflecting strong waves.

40 Beach nourishment builds up beaches to break up incoming waves – it works with natural processes and looks more natural and so has less visual impact.

>> Weather and climate

41 Weather describes the daily condition of the atmosphere in a place; climate describes the average weather conditions over a period of time.

42 Warm/hot dry weather

43 Arctic and polar maritime air masses

44 Depressions – low-pressure weather systems bringing unsettled/changeable weather (cloud, wind and rain); anticyclones – high-pressure weather systems in which air is sinking, usually bringing settled, drier weather

45 Sinking air in anticyclonic weather can prevent air pollution from dispersing.

46 Cold environments are located in the far northern hemisphere and in the Antarctic region.

47 Cold environments are used for resource exploration and extraction e.g. drilling for oil in Alaska and for tourism e.g. expeditions to Antarctica.

48 The Antarctic Treaty sets aside Antarctica as a place of science and peace. Mining is banned, fishing is controlled and all waste must be removed from the continent.

49 Hot deserts are found around the Tropics of Cancer and Capricorn.

50 Desertification is the degradation of dry land and the spread of desert conditions.

51 Humans have emitted high levels of greenhouse gases (carbon dioxide, methane and nitrous oxides) which trap and reflect much of the wave energy radiating from the Earth, keeping temperatures higher. This is causing the Earth to warm up.

>> Ecosystems

52 Biotic – living parts of an ecosystem (plants and animals); abiotic – non-living parts of an ecosystem (soil, water)

53 Decomposers break down waste or dead matter from plants and animals, returning nutrients to an ecosystem via the soil.

54 Dead matter decomposes rapidly in the hot and wet conditions.

55 To use the land for logging, mining, cattle ranching and cash-crop plantations

56 Deforestation removes the supply of nutrients through new humus, and the heavy rainfall means that nutrients are rapidly leached from the soil.

57 Sustainable logging can be implemented, protected areas can be established, people can be educated about the importance of the rainforest and mining companies can be required to replant trees once they have finished mining an area.

Topic checker answers

>> Population

58 Birth rates are high but death rates are declining due to improvements in healthcare and sanitation, leading to a rapid rise in population.

59 Lower infant mortality, use of birth control, rising prosperity, improvements in education, government policies

60 LEDCs have broader based pyramids due to higher birth rates and are narrower at the top due to lower life expectancy; MEDCs have a narrower base due to lower birth rates and are broader at the top due to higher life expectancy.

61 Due to low birth rates and small family sizes; could lead to large elderly populations needing to be supported by a smaller working population

62 Push – negative reasons persuading people to leave an area; pull – positive reasons attracting people to move to a new area

63 Someone who has been forced to leave their home

>> Urban settlement

64 LEDCs

65 Heavy industry (e.g. manufacturing) moved away from many inner-city areas during the second half of the twentieth century. Jobs were lost and many people became unemployed. Old industrial buildings became derelict and the surrounding area run down.

66 Many inner-city areas have been redeveloped and regenerated. Redevelopment has involved clearing land (removing old buildings etc.) and building homes, new shops and offices. The aim of this is to attract new investment into the area and makes it a more attractive place to live. This improves the economy and is known as regeneration.

67 Unplanned settlements often built illegally and at very high densities by the very poor (usually migrants) in cities in LEDCs

68 Self-help schemes involve the squatter populations improving their housing conditions and provision of basic services by providing cheap materials and low interest loans; site-and-service schemes provide building plots and services needed (roads, drainage, clean water, electricity and, in some cases, education and health services).

69 Eco-towns are sustainable urban areas. They aim to promote social, economic and environmental sustainability (creating jobs for all, dealing effectively with waste, generating renewable energy and improving access to essential services). There are ten eco-towns planned for England.

70 Traffic calming slows down traffic and may involve using speed bumps or narrowing a road. Traffic calming is aimed at making roads safer and preventing large vehicles entering certain areas of a town or city.

>> The changing countryside

71 A green belt is an area of land found around the edge of a town or city. The land is protected from development and is intended to stop the town or city growing outwards into the countryside.

72 Counter-urbanisation is the movement of people from urban areas to the countryside – urban–rural migration.

73 Counter-urbanisation can cause conflicts between new residents and existing residents. Sometimes services in the rural area may be affected by counter-urbanisation and some shops may have to close. This is because the new migrants tend to work away from the village and therefore do not spend much time or money in the local area.

74 Employment in farming in MEDCs is declining. This is due to the mechanisation of farming (use of machines).

75 Farmers can reduce the impact of farming on the environment by carrying out organic farming, restoring hedgerows and creating wildlife corridors. They can also apply for grants from the EU for environmental projects.

76 Subsistence farmers grow crops and raise animals to support their families and/or communities. They do not farm for profit. Yields are low and their methods are low-tech.

77 The Green Revolution involved using high-yield crop varieties to increase food production and meet growing demand.

>> The global economy

78 Globalisation involves people and places becoming more connected.

79 TNCs are transnational corporations. They operate beyond national boundaries (i.e. all over the world).

80	Primary, secondary, tertiary and quaternary industry
81	MEDCs tend to have low levels of primary employment. The majority of people are employed in tertiary industry. The quaternary sector is often growing.
82	LEDCs tend to have high levels of primary employment. Some people work in tertiary industry. The secondary sector is often growing.
83	This is the quaternary sector and involves people working in research and development and consultancy. The sector is very reliant on specialist knowledge and technology.
84	Thailand, Malaysia, Philippines, Indonesia and China

>> An unequal world

85	List may include: end hunger, universal education for all, gender equality, child health, maternal health, combating HIV/Aids, environmental sustainability, global partnership
86	The difference between the value of a country's imports and exports
87	It will be vulnerable to changes in demand and world prices for the products; if demand or prices fall, they will lose income and not have alternative sources of income to fall back on; if they rely on the export of agricultural products, they could suffer if there are bad harvests or environmental problems
88	Bilateral, multilateral and non-governmental aid
89	Often use expensive and complex technology increasing dependence on overseas suppliers; not always appropriate for solving the problems of local people; decisions often imposed from outside and don't involve local people
90	Grassroots development involves making small changes to an area and working with local people and local skills. It is sometimes called bottom-up development.

>> Tourism

91	More people with higher disposable incomes and longer paid holidays; improvements in transport
92	To give the public access to attractive rural environments, while preserving the landscape and looking after the interests of local people and the local economy

93	Valuable source of foreign earnings; profits to fund other developments (transport, education, health and welfare); increasing awareness and understanding of other cultures and places
94	Environmental impacts (construction of hotels, transport routes, demand for water, pollution from sewage, etc.); cultural impact of mass tourism; concentration of benefits in tourist areas
95	Sustainable tourism makes use of natural resources without long-term damage to the environment
96	More sustainable; smaller numbers cause less damage to the environment; less negative impact on local culture and communities; local communities benefit more from income from tourism; income can be used to improve health and education; encourages conservation of wildlife and the environment

>> Sustainable development

97	Development that meets the needs of the present without compromising the ability of future generations to meet their own needs.
98	Reduce, reuse, recycle
99	Renewable – can be used again to produce energy; non-renewable – cannot be replaced once used up
100	High levels of air pollution (e.g. CO_2) contributing to global warming; dangers involved in extraction (mining)
101	Cleaner (less pollution), more efficient (low waste) and easier to transport than other fuels
102	When fossil fuels are burnt, sulphur dioxide (SO_2) and nitrogen oxide (NO_2) are released as pollution; sunlight converts these gases into sulphuric acid and nitric acid, which dissolve in moisture in the atmosphere, resulting in acidic rainfall.
103	Noise pollution and the visual impacts of large wind turbines; variable strength of winds
104	Water stress is when the demand for water exceeds supply.
105	The UK authorities manage water supplies using advertising campaigns, installing water meters and imposing hosepipe bans during the summer months.

Using maps 1

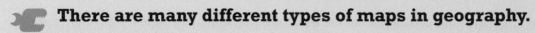
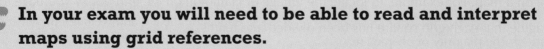
A Types of map

1 Here are some of the different types of maps that may appear in your exam.

> **Sketch maps**: These are simple maps that are drawn quickly and not usually to scale.
>
> **Statistical maps**: These are maps that show statistical information e.g. birth rates in different countries of the world. A common statistical map is a **choropleth map**. This type of map uses shading to show different values or groups of values. This choropleth map shows population density.
>
> World population
>
> Tropic of Cancer
>
> Equator
>
> Tropic of Capricorn
>
> ■ High density   ■ Moderately density   ■ Low density
>
> **Ordnance Survey maps (OS maps)**: These are detailed maps produced for the UK. They come in a standard format

2 The rest of this section focuses on Ordnance Survey (OS) maps as most GCSE geography examinations include at least one question based on an OS map. However, the skills explained here are relevant to nearly all maps.

B Grid references

1 Grid references are used to help people locate places or features on a map.

2 **key fact** Grid references can be given in two ways: four-figure grid references and six-figure grid references.

3 **Four-figure grid references** are used to locate a single grid square.

For example, to locate 0722 on the grid opposite, you have to:

- Begin reading the map from the bottom left-hand corner.

- Read the numbers along the bottom of the map first.

- Move along the bottom row of numbers until you reach the number 07.

- The number 07 is found on the left side of the grid square.

- Now read the numbers on the side of the map.

- Move up the side of the map until you reach the number 22, which is at the bottom of the grid square.

- You will notice that an L-shape is formed in the bottom left-hand corner of grid square 0722.

> **remember >>**
>
> Grid references are a bit like coordinates, which you will have used in maths.

④ **Six-figure grid references** are used to locate the exact position of a place or feature within a grid square on a map. For example, to locate the village of Hampton on the grid below you have to:

- Imagine that each grid square has been divided into tenths.

- Again, read the map from the bottom left-hand corner.

- Move along the bottom row of numbers until you reach the left-hand side of the square with Hampton in it. The exact position of Hampton is 06 and 3 tenths.

- Now move up the side of the grid until you reach the bottom of the grid square with the village of Hampton in it. The exact position of Hampton is 22 and 7 tenths.

- The six-figure grid reference for Hampton is 063227.

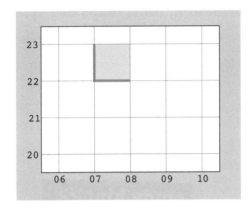

Four-figure grid reference

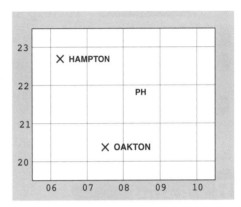

Six-figure grid reference

C Scale

① **key fact** **The scale of a map helps you to work out the distance between one place and another.**

② On an OS map, scale is shown using a **scale line**, usually found at the bottom of the map or with the key.

③ In an exam, you are likely to be given an OS map with a scale of 1:25 000 or 1:50 000. On a 1:50 000 map, 1 cm represents 50 000 cm.

>> practice questions

1 Using the map above, give the four-figure grid reference for the village of Oakton.

2 Using the map above, give the six-figure grid reference for the village of Oakton.

Using maps 2

 Understanding a map can also involve using map symbols and interpreting contour lines.

A Map symbols

key fact To help show detailed information, most maps use symbols.

2. Map symbols are explained using a **key**. The key gives you the meaning of each symbol.

3. Different types of map may use different symbols. However, there are some common symbols that are used on most maps.

4. OS maps have a set of standard symbols. The OS map in this book has a key (page 131). If you are given an OS map in an exam, it will have a similar key attached. Make sure you use it to help you read and understand the map.

B Relief

key fact Relief is the shape of the land. Studying relief involves looking at the height of the land.

study hint >>
Contour lines in a V indicate a valley and circular contours indicate a hill.

2. **Relief** is shown on a map using contour lines or spot heights.

3. **Contour lines** are brown lines that show the height of the land. The height of the land along a contour line is measured in metres above sea level.

- Contour lines join up points of equal height above sea level. The height of the land is the same at any point along one single contour line.

- Each contour line goes up in set intervals. On a 1:50 000 map, each line goes up 10 metres.

- The closer together the contour lines, the steeper the relief of the land; the further apart the contour lines, the gentler the relief.

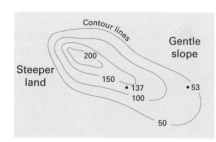

4. **Spot heights** are shown on a map as a dot, with the height of the land at that point written beside it.

study hint >>
Can you draw and identify common OS map symbols?

exam tip >>
Drawing a simple sketch map to illustrate a case study is a useful exam technique. Sketch maps are quick to draw and can be labelled to show information about a place.

Ordnance Survey map of Newport, South Wales

>> practice questions

Use the map of Newport above to answer the following questions:

1 Name the farm found in square 3585.

2 Name the features found at: a) 365829   b) 381834   c) 362878.

3 What is the height of the land at 388881?

Using images and analysing data

- Geographers often use images and statistics to help them understand people and places.

- Analysing statistics can help us identify patterns or trends.

- Geographical data is often shown in the form of a graph or chart.

A Using images

① key fact Images are often used in geography. These images may include photographs, artists' impressions or satellite images.

② If a photograph is used in an exam question, it will have been included for a reason. Consider why the photograph has been used and assess what information the examiner wants you to pick out from the picture.

The photograph below shows tourism development along the Mediterranean coast. It has been labelled to show key information about such resorts.

The hotels are **clustered** together to form a resort.

Around the tourist resort the **landscape** is relatively undeveloped and open.

Water sports are common in coastal resorts. They attract tourists, but they can also damage the environment through pollution. Vibrations and noise from the engines of boats may disturb animal wildlife.

High-rise hotel developments are very different in style to the traditional buildings found in the area. Many local governments in the region now have planning laws that regulate the height of hotels and other buildings.

Many hotels have **swimming pools**. They attract tourists to areas with warm climates, such as the Mediterranean, but they use a lot of water, which can drain local water supplies.

Roads are needed to connect the tourist resort with other settlements and the airport.

B Analysing data and statistics

1 **key fact** Geographers often use statistical data to identify patterns or trends.

2 Using statistics involves analysing numbers and figures (e.g. birth rates or death rates).

3 You are likely to be given relatively simple statistical data in your GCSE exam. You will be expected to understand and interpret the data you are given.

4 Data and statistics are usually shown in the form of a graph, chart or table.

5 In your exam, you may be asked to add information to a graph.

C Working with graphs

1 **key fact** Geographers use a range of different graphs to show data.

- **Line graphs** show change over time. Time is usually shown on the x-axis. An example of a line graph can be seen on page 76.

- **Bar graphs** make use of shaded bars of different lengths to show the value of a particular item of data. Population pyramids (see page 77) and climate graphs (see page 52) make use of these bars.

- **Pie charts** and **divided bar charts** show percentages (see page 99).

- **Scatter graphs** show the relationship between two sets of data. They show how two sets of data correlate (link) with each other. You should not join up the points on a scatter graph; instead, you can add a line of best fit.

- **Triangular graphs** have three axes and they are used to show percentages. The most common use of a triangular graph is to show a country's employment structure (see page 99).

2 If you are asked to describe the pattern on a graph in an exam, make sure you quote figures from the graph in your answer.

> **remember >>**
> Learn the names of the two axes on a graph. The x-axis is horizontal. The y-axis is vertical ('y to the sky!').

> **remember >>**
> When describing the pattern on a graph, quote figures and use descriptive words such as *rises, falls, declines, grows, rapidly* or *steadily*. Look for exceptions to the pattern shown.

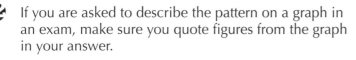

>> practice questions

1. List three land uses shown in the photograph opposite.

2. Using the photograph on the opposite page, give two reasons why people may want to visit the Mediterranean coast.

3. Use evidence from the photograph on the opposite page to describe the effects of tourism on people and the environment.

Using new technologies in geography

⟫ **Technology plays an important part in geography.**

⟫ **Satellite technology, GPS and GIS are all examples of how technology can help geographers to find out more about people and places.**

A Using technology in geography

① **key fact** **Geographers often make use of technology to help them find out about people and places.**

② The Internet can help geographers carry out research. Data published on websites are a useful source of secondary data. However, it is important to ask critical questions about the data you read on the Internet: where have the data come from? Who provided it and why? If you are using research from the Internet in your classwork or a controlled assessment task, make sure you state which website you got the information from.

③ Technology can help to monitor, record and forecast the weather. This technology may be part of a weather station. A weather station includes a variety of equipment needed to record different elements of the weather (e.g. temperature, rainfall, wind speed and wind direction). Weather stations are found all over the world. The data can be sent to a computer, where it is collated and analysed.

④ Satellite and space technology can help provide us with images of the Earth. This is called remote sensing. The data collected can be stored, manipulated and analysed using computers. Satellite images and specialised digital photographs can be produced to show what is going on in areas that are dangerous or difficult to reach (e.g. Antarctica). They can be used to show the impacts of climate change (e.g. melting glaciers) or rates of deforestation (e.g. in the Amazon rainforest). Satellite images can also help us understand and forecast the weather.

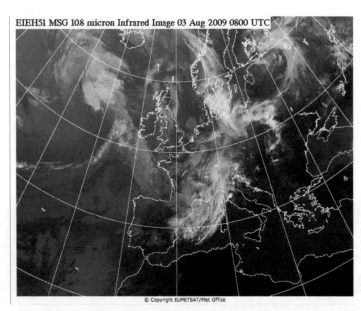

EIEH51 MSG 10.8 micron Infrared Image 03 Aug 2009 0800 UTC

© Copyright EUMETSAT/Met Office

Satellite image of Europe

⑤ The Global Positioning System (GPS) is a navigation system that uses satellites to help pinpoint locations on Earth. GPS receiver units pick up radiowave signals from the satellites. These radiowaves tell the device exactly where it is on Earth. GPS can also be used for navigation and map-making.

study hint >>

When completing homework or controlled assessment tasks, think about ways in which you can make use of technology such as GPS.

B Geographic Information Systems (GIS)

① **key fact** Geographic Information Systems (GIS) are systems that store, analyse, edit and display geographical data. These data usually relate to a particular location.

② GIS brings together remote sensing, digital photography, GPS and Internet technology.

③ A common use of GIS is to develop detailed and sometimes interactive maps.

④ Maps are created by adding layers of information to a base map.

⑤ An example of a simple GIS is Google Maps or Google Earth. Both these systems allow users to construct maps which display information. Photographs or text can be added and satellite images displayed.

>> practice questions

1 Using the satellite image on the opposite page, describe the cloud cover over Europe.

2 Name three groups of people who may find using GIS useful.
For each group, say how GIS can help them.

Tectonic hazards 1

- The Earth is made up of four layers: the inner core, outer core, mantle and crust.

- The Earth's crust is broken into sections called 'plates'.

- A plate boundary is the point where two plates meet.

- Most earthquakes and volcanoes occur on or close to plate boundaries.

A The structure of the Earth

1 key fact The Earth is made up of four layers.

Crust
The thinnest layer of the Earth is made up of solid rock. The crust is the outer layer of the Earth, like the skin of an apple.

Mantle
The largest section of the Earth is made up of semi-molten rock. These partially melted rocks are called magma. Temperatures here are around 5000 °C.

Outer core
This is made up of liquid iron and nickel.

Inner core
The centre of the Earth is made of solid iron and nickel. This is the hottest part of the Earth, with temperatures of around 5500 °C.

2 The Earth's crust is broken up into pieces called plates, which move or 'float' on the mantle.

3 Heat rises and falls in the mantle creating currents. These are called convection currents. Convection currents cause the Earth's plates to move. The plates move very slowly (around one or two millimetres a year).

4 The movement of the Earth's plates is known as tectonic activity.

B The Earth's plates

1 key fact The movement of the Earth's plates causes earthquakes and volcanoes.

2 The map opposite shows the world's main tectonic plates. The point at which two plates meet is called a plate boundary.

3 Most of the world's earthquake and volcano zones are found on or close to plate boundaries.

4 The Earth's plates move in different directions. The direction of plate movement is shown on the map using arrows.

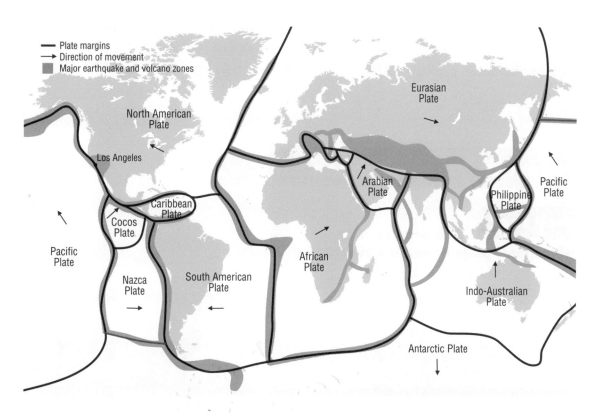

C Plate boundaries

>> **key fact** There are three main types of plate boundary.

remember >>
The processes that take place inside the Earth often have an influence on what happens on the Earth's surface.

1 At a **constructive plate boundary**, two plates move apart from each other.

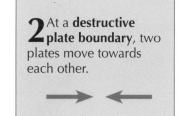

2 At a **destructive plate boundary**, two plates move towards each other.

3 At a **conservative plate boundary**, two plates slide past each other.

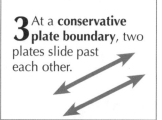

>> practice questions

1 Use the map to name a plate that is moving northwards.

2 Use the map to describe the distribution of earthquakes or volcanoes.

3 Name the two plates that form a constructive plate boundary.

Tectonic hazards 2

- There are three main types of plate boundary: constructive, destructive and conservative.

- At some plate boundaries, new land is created; at others, it is destroyed.

- The movement of the plates causes earthquakes, volcanoes and tsunamis.

A Constructive plate boundaries

>> **key fact** At a constructive, or divergent, plate boundary, two plates move apart from each other.

- As the plates move apart, semi-molten rock called magma rises through the gap in the Earth's crust and cools down to form new crust.

- An example of a constructive plate boundary is the Mid-Atlantic Ridge. Here, a chain of underwater volcanoes has formed along the plate boundary.

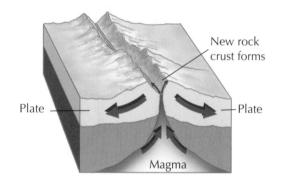

New rock crust forms

Plate

Plate

Magma

B Destructive plate boundaries

① **key fact** At a destructive, or convergent, plate boundary, two plates move towards each other.

② When an oceanic plate moves towards a continental plate, the denser oceanic plate is forced underneath the continental plate in a process called subduction.

③ **key fact** The oceanic crust melts, creating magma. The magma rises to form volcanoes.

④ At a destructive plate boundary, the movement of the plates may push the continental crust upward to form fold mountains. This process is called folding.

⑤ Earthquakes are common here. They occur in the subduction zone.

Land (continental crust)

Trench

Oceanic crust

New mountains form

Plate

Plate

Subduction zone

Volcanoes may form

C   Conservative plate boundaries

① **key fact** At a conservative, or transform, boundary, the plates move horizontally past each other, without creating or destroying the Earth's crust.

② An example of a conservative boundary is the San Andreas Fault, USA.

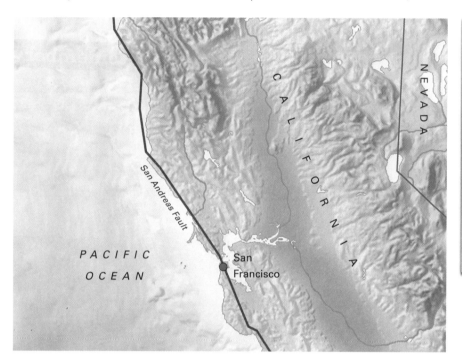

exam tip >>

People use different names for the different types of plate boundary. Find out which ones you are likely to see in your exam and learn these.

D   Tectonic hazards

① Tectonic hazards can occur at each of the different types of plate boundary.

② A hazard is something that has the potential to cause harm. Volcanoes, earthquakes and tsunamis are tectonic hazards.

③ Earthquakes can occur at each of the different types of plate boundary. Volcanoes occur at constructive and destructive boundaries.

④ Volcanic eruptions at destructive boundaries can be very explosive. An extremely large volcano is sometimes called a supervolcano. If they erupt, the impacts can be enormous.

exam tip >>

You could be asked to explain what happens at a particular type of plate boundary. Use a simple diagram to help your explanation (even if you are not asked to).

>> practice questions

1 **Name a destructive plate boundary. Use the map on page 11 to help you.**

2 **Using geographical terms, explain what happens at a destructive plate boundary.**

3 **Explain what is meant by the term 'folding'.**

Earthquakes

Earthquakes are caused when one of the Earth's plates gets stuck. When the plates jolt free, pressure is released as waves of energy.

Earthquakes tend to have a greater impact in Less Economically Developed Countries (LEDCs).

A What are earthquakes?

1 **key fact** The movement of the Earth's plates can cause earthquakes.

2 **key fact** Plates do not move smoothly. Sometimes a plate gets stuck. Pressure builds up and, when this pressure is released, an earthquake can occur.

3 The point below the Earth's surface where the pressure is released is called the focus.

4 The point on the Earth's surface directly above the focus is called the epicentre.

5 Shock waves are produced when pressure is released from the focus. These waves are called seismic waves. The seismic waves are strongest at the epicentre of an earthquake. This is where the most damage is caused during an earthquake. The seismic waves spread out from the focus like ripples on a pond. As they travel outwards, they lose energy.

remember >>
Earthquakes can occur at any type of plate boundary.

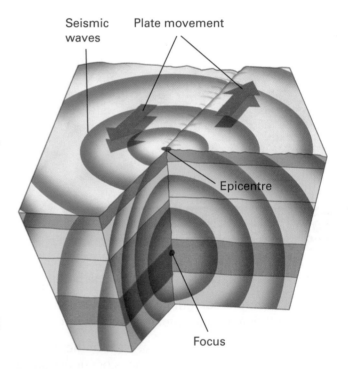

Seismic waves

Plate movement

Epicentre

Focus

B Measuring earthquakes

1 The strength of an earthquake is recorded using a machine called a seismometer.

The seismometer picks up vibrations and tremors during an earthquake and produces a seismograph to show the strength of the Earth's movements.

2 The strength or magnitude of an earthquake is measured using the Richter scale.

C The effects of an earthquake

1 **key fact** Earthquakes can have a devastating effect on people and the environment.

- The immediate or primary effects of an earthquake include the collapse of buildings, roads and railways. People may be killed or injured and property damaged.

- The long-term or secondary effects of an earthquake include gas explosions and fires. Communications can fail, with telephone lines and computer links cut. Water can become contaminated as sewage and clean water pipes fracture.
A lack of clean water can lead to the spread of disease.

remember >>

It is more difficult for LEDCs to prepare for earthquakes due to limited capital and resources.

2 **key fact** Natural disasters such as earthquakes tend to have a greater impact on LEDCs than MEDCs.

Buildings in LEDCs are not always strong enough to withstand the damage caused by earthquakes. LEDCs do not have sufficient healthcare facilities to deal with emergency situations. Access and communications in LEDCs tend to be poor. It is difficult to warn people about possible dangers or bring them emergency supplies. LEDCs also have limited money and resources to rebuild areas that are damaged.

D Preparing for earthquakes

1 It is difficult to predict earthquakes. A seismometer can be used to monitor tremors inside the Earth's crust and therefore identify potential earthquakes. However, earthquake predictions are not accurate enough to rely on. It is more worthwhile to invest money and resources in preparing for earthquakes.

2 There are many things that people can do to prepare for an earthquake:

Training people to deal with an earthquake emergency (e.g. earthquake drills in schools).	Encouraging people to keep an earthquake kit at home, including first-aid items, tinned food and a radio.
Roads and buildings can be constructed to reduce the damage caused by an earthquake (e.g. electronic shutters to cover windows).	Buildings can be constructed to be earthquake-proof. The building absorbs some of the energy released during the earthquake.

>> practice questions

1 Explain what is meant by:

  a) the focus of an earthquake   b) the epicentre of an earthquake.

2 Explain why the impact of an earthquake tends to be worse in LEDCs than in MEDCs.

3 With reference to a named example, describe the effects of an earthquake on the people living in an earthquake zone.

Volcanoes

 Volcanoes can form at both constructive and destructive plate boundaries.

 There are two main types of volcano: cone and shield.

A The formation of volcanoes

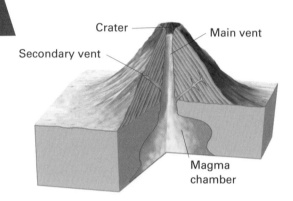

Crater — Main vent
Secondary vent
Magma chamber

1 Volcanoes are formed when semi-molten rock called magma forces its way to the surface through weaknesses in the crust. As the magma rises, the surface pressure builds up within the Earth causing a volcanic explosion.

2 When the magma reaches the surface of the Earth, it becomes lava.

B Types of volcano

Volcanoes can be classified (grouped) in a number of different ways.

1 One way of classifying volcanoes is to look at their shape and composition.

Cone volcanoes – Tend to be found at destructive plate boundaries. Tall and steep-sided. Formed by acid lava, which is thick and viscous (sticky). The acid lava flows slowly and hardens quickly. This explains the steep-sided shape of these volcanoes. Erupt violently throwing out steam, gas and lava bombs.

Thick lava
Tall narrow cone
Steep slope

Shield volcanoes – Tend to be found at constructive plate boundaries. Low with gentle slopes. Formed by basic lava, which is thin and runny. Basic lava spreads quickly to form low, shield-shaped volcanoes. Erupt frequently and gently.

Fluid lava
Low wide cone
Gentle slope

Composite volcanoes are made up of alternating layers of lava and ash. Other volcanoes are made from lava only.

Lava   Ash

2 Another way of classifying volcanoes is to look at how likely they are to erupt.

Active: a volcano that has erupted recently and is considered likely to erupt again (e.g. the Nyiragongo volcano in the Democratic Republic of Congo, Africa – last erupted January 2002)

Types of volcano

Dormant: a volcano that has erupted within the last two thousand years but is not currently active (e.g. Mount Vesuvius in Italy)

Extinct: a volcano that is not considered likely to erupt again

C — What are the effects of a volcanic eruption?

>> **key fact** Volcanic eruptions can have a devastating effect on people and the environment. Lives can be lost and landscapes destroyed.

Hot blasts of gas are sent into the atmosphere at the beginning of a volcanic eruption.

Lava flows can destroy settlements (towns, cities and villages) and clear areas of natural vegetation, such as woodland.

Ash is thrown high into the atmosphere and covers the surrounding landscape as it settles. Sometimes ash remains in the atmosphere for several days and it can travel thousands of miles before settling on the Earth's surface.

The impact of a volcanic eruption

The heat of the volcanic eruption can melt snow and ice, causing fast-moving mud flows called **lahars**.

When a volcano explodes, lava bombs can be thrown into the air. These are made up of pieces of rock and ash.

Like earthquakes, volcanoes can have **primary** and **secondary impacts**.

D — Why do people live in areas of volcanic activity?

Although volcanoes can be very dangerous, many people continue to live near them, often in very large numbers (high densities). Volcanoes can bring people many benefits:

✓ The ash deposited during a volcanic eruption adds valuable nutrients to the soils and helps to fertilise it. This helps agriculture and farming.

✓ Volcanic landscapes are very attractive and attract tourists. This brings in valuable income to the area.

✓ In volcanic areas, electricity can be generated from geothermal energy.

✓ Although many people choose to live near volcanoes, some people are too poor to leave their home (particularly in LEDCs). Even if someone can afford to leave the area, they may be attached to their home and surroundings. Many people have to be forced to leave if a volcano becomes dangerous – they don't want to leave their home.

remember >>

Volcanoes and earthquakes do not happen only in LEDCs. North America is also affected by natural hazards.

>> practice questions

1 **Describe how a volcano is formed.**

2 **Using named examples, explain why many people live in areas of volcanic activity.**

exam tip >>

If you are writing about geographical processes in your exam, make sure you use the correct terms and refer to places you have studied.

Case study
The Sichuan earthquake, China

 The earthquake happened at a collision boundary.

 The severity of the earthquake was increased by the shallow epicentre, only 19 km below ground.

 It will take many years to repair the damage caused by this earthquake.

A Causes of the earthquake

- The earthquake struck 92 km northwest of the city of Chengdu in eastern Sichuan Province over 1500 km from Beijing at 2.28 pm on 12 May 2008.

- It measured 7.9 on the Richter scale.

- The earthquake happened along the Longmenshan fault at the boundary of the Indo-Australian Plate and the Eurasian Plate, which were moving towards each other at a rate of 5 cm/year, resulting in the uplift of the Himalaya and Tibetan plateaux and massive seismic activity.

Damage caused by the earthquake in Sichuan Province, China

B Effects of the earthquake

- It killed 69 172 people and injured a further 375 000. Over 45 million people were affected by it. Even the New World Tower in Hong Kong was evacuated.

- 15 million have been forced to move.

- 15 million buildings collapsed (about 80% of the total in the area) including 7000 schools in Sichuan Province. 5 million lost their homes.

- 5000 km of pipes were destroyed.

- 100 000 hectares of rice fields were damaged as irrigation pipes were broken.

- 12 million animals perished, including 1 million pigs.

- In Shifang, the collapse of two chemical factories leaked liquid ammonia into the local area, killing hundreds.

- 900 school children were killed when a school collapsed in Dujiangyan.

- China Mobile had 2300 base stations suspended.

- 391 dams were damaged.

- Insurers estimate losses at US$1 billion and damages at $20 billion.

- By 27 May 2008, 34 quake lakes had formed due to landslides blocking and damming rivers. The most threatening quake lake at Tangjiashan mountain led to the evacuation of 200 000 people downstream at Mianyang.

- On 27 May, an aftershock led to the collapse of 420 000 buildings.

C Responses to the earthquake

- On the day of the emergency, the National Disaster Relief Commission initiated a Level 1 emergency contingency plan and the government allocated 27 million yuan (£2 million) for disaster relief. The Prime Minister, Wen Jiabao, flew to the earthquake zone.

- On the day of the emergency, 10 medical teams and 50 000 troops were dispatched to Wenchuan County, as well as an emergency relief team of 184 people.

- The Red Cross Society of China facilitated the supply of tents, water, food and medicine to remote rural areas cut off by rock and landslides. These were dropped by helicopter.

- On 13 May, China accepted help from the outside world. Aid was accepted from the Tzu Chi Foundation and Red Cross of Taiwan. The UK gave £1 million and rescue teams flew in from South Korea and Russia. The US shared some of its satellite images of the earthquake area and dropped generators and tents into affected areas.

- On 15 May, a further 90 helicopters were deployed in relief operations.

- On 6 November 2008, the central government announced spending of 1 trillion yuan (about US$146.5 billion) over the next three years to rebuild areas ravaged by the earthquake.

D Why was there so much damage?

1. The epicentre of the earthquake was shallow, only 19 km below ground. This allowed the seismic waves to travel the short distance to the surface without losing much power.

2. The firmness of the terrain allows the seismic waves to travel a longer distance without losing power.

3. The area is densely populated.

4. Many of the houses in the rural areas were built of mud and collapsed.

5. Schools collapsed due to construction flaws and a lack of building regulations.

study hint >>

Practise labelling photographs to identify and describe earthquake damage.

>> practice questions

1. Describe the effects of the Sichuan earthquake on people and the environment.

2. Explain why the area is vulnerable to earthquakes.

exam tip >>

Good answers will evaluate the quality of the human response to the earthquake hazard.

Case study
The Mt Nyiragongo volcano, Congo

 The volcano happened at a constructive plate boundary.

 Mt Nyiragongo is part of the chain of volcanoes in the African Rift Valley.

 It is a very active volcano.

A Causes of the volcano

- Mt Nyiragongo is in the Democratic Republic of Congo in Central Africa, near the border with Rwanda. It lies on a constructive plate boundary where the two parts of the African Plate are pulling apart along a fault line. This causes the volcano to erupt frequently.

- On 17 January 2002, there was a large eruption on the southern side of the mountain which spewed out a river of hot, runny basalt lava 1000 metres wide and 2 metres deep. This lava flowed very quickly at 150 km per hour to the city of Goma 20 km away.

Mt Nyiragongo: view into the lava lake

B Effects of the volcano

- The volcano triggered several earthquakes which measured 5 on the Richter scale and damaged buildings.

- 147 people died from gas fumes and getting trapped in the lava.

- 40% of Goma was destroyed, including 1200 metres of the airport runway and the hospitals. Power and water supplies were cut off.

- 12 500 homes were destroyed.

- 120 000 people were left homeless.

- Thousands of people were injured from smoke and fumes and contracted dysentery.

- 350 000 evacuated the area. Most fled as refugees to Gisenyi in Rwanda.

- Abandoned buildings were looted.

- Lake Kivu was polluted by sulphurous lava which contaminated water supplies and increased the temperature of the lake, killing aquatic life.

C Reponses to the volcano

- The government issued a Red Alert for Goma and the area around it before the volcano happened. This meant a full evacuation happened.

- In the first week, the United Nations sent aid to assist the homeless, including 260 tonnes of food consisting of biscuits, maize, cooking oil and beans.

- Oxfam set up camps to shelter people and provide clean water and some sanitation.

- The total cost of the aid was US$15 million.

- The UK Disasters Emergency Committee appealed for donations.

- World governments donated $35 million to help to rebuild Goma.

- The World Health Organisation gave emergency vaccinations.

- The United Nations developed a one-year recovery programme with a budget of $4.9 million. This was spent on shelter through resettlement, livelihood restoration, strengthening disaster preparedness and mitigation process.

D Why do people still live near the volcano?

1. Mt Nyiragongo is still active, yet most of the refugees have returned to their homes. This is because most are too poor to move anywhere else and have family and tribal links to the area going back generations. Many are farmers and live on the slopes of the mountains and benefit from the fertile soils of the weathered lava.

2. Lake Kivu provides a supply of fresh water and people can make a living from fishing on the lake.

3. The cooled lava contains valuable minerals which can be extracted.

4. Some people may not be aware of the risk.

5. As geoscientists can predict volcanic eruptions, people can easily be evacuated when an eruption is imminent.

study hint >>

Divide effects into the impacts on people and on the environment.

>> practice questions

1 Explain why the volcano happened.

2 What were the short-term and long-term responses to the volcano hazard?

3 Why do people still live near Goma?

exam tip >>

Located detail is important in case study answers.

Tropical storms

 Extreme low-pressure weather conditions create hazards such as hurricanes.

 With global warming, more hurricanes are likely.

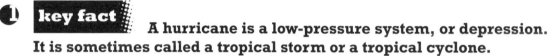
A Causes of tropical storms

key fact A hurricane is a low-pressure system, or depression. It is sometimes called a tropical storm or a tropical cyclone.

1. Hurricanes develop in the tropics above a warm sea (over 27 °C) and move away from the equator westwards.

2. Hurricanes happen when the weather is hottest. This is between May and November in the Northern hemisphere and November and April in the Southern hemisphere.

3. Areas vulnerable to hurricanes include: the Indian subcontinent, Southeast Asia, Central America and the Caribbean.

4. A hurricane can stretch up to 800 km in diameter and be up to 20 km in height.

remember >>

Hurricanes are low pressure systems and form over oceans in the tropics.

- The eye of the storm is made up of very low pressure and gives calm weather.

- Either side of the vortex, low pressure encourages air to rise and cool, clouds to form and rain to fall. The lower the pressure, the faster the winds, often over 200 km/h.

- Hurricanes weaken and blow themselves out when they meet land as they are cut off from the warm sea, which is their main source of energy.

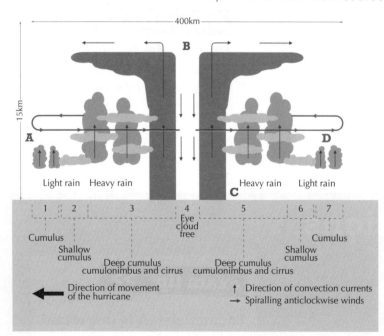

A Warm moist air rises and forms cumulus clouds. Trade winds sweep in below, creating a spiral.

B Winds of over 200 mph flow out of the top of the hurricane.

C Bands of rain spiral in towards the eye of the hurricane. Heaviest rain at the wall of the eye.

D The spiral forms a giant Catherine wheel, with winds of 200 mph near the centre.

Sequence of weather

1 Sky becomes cloudy, wind increases, sea gets choppy

2 Cumulus clouds build up, light rain, strong winds with gusts, heavy seas

3 Towering cumulonimbus clouds, heavy rain, strong winds and very rough seas

4 Clear skies, warmer, no clouds or winds

5 Towering cumulonimbus clouds again, heavy rain, strongest winds from different direction due to spiralling, very rough seas

6 Lighter rain, wind speeds decrease, with gusts, rough seas

7 Sky clearer, wind speeds decrease, seas calmer

B Effects of tropical storms

1 People and animals are drowned in the storm surge and flooding from the rain.

2 Strong winds destroy buildings, farmland, power and communications and transport. How bad the damage is depends on how strong both the wind and the buildings are.

3 Flooding is caused by heavy rainfall and storm surges. There are landslides as hills become saturated and sometimes tornadoes cause damage.

C Coping with tropical storms

1 Advances in technology have improved the ability of more economically developed countries (MEDCs) to predict and monitor the path of tropical storms. Satellite images are used to gather information about the size and strength of tropical storms. Despite this, it is difficult for scientists to predict exactly where a tropical storm will hit land and how strong it will be. This is why, in 2005, Hurricane Katrina took top US meteorologists by surprise.

2 These advances in technology mean local and national governments can give out evacuation warnings up to two days in advance and set up emergency shelters. This cannot stop damage to buildings but is the main way to avoid deaths in high-intensity tropical storms.

3 In less economically developed countries (LEDCs), these expensive methods of monitoring tropical storms may not be available. Countries such as Bangladesh have built many cyclone shelters in vulnerable zones to provide a safe haven for local people. These buildings are built at a height of 7 m above ground and are made to withstand a potential storm surge.

4 People are encouraged to have a family plan, a disaster kit, a place to go and to secure their home. The family plan should include an assessment of the risk of each hurricane hazard and escape routes from home. The disaster kit should include such things as water, food, clothing and flashlights. The shutters and doors of homes should be properly secured with bolts, while the frame joists should be strapped together.

5 Efforts are being concentrated on reducing the impact of the storm surge, as the flat landscapes by the coast offer little protection. People are now starting to plant mangrove trees in specific areas to serve as a natural barrier against the water. Cyclone walls are being built along river banks to protect against a surge.

6 Scientists are predicting that increases in sea-level temperature due to global warming may cause more tropical storms of greater intensity. This, combined with rising sea levels, will place low-lying places such as Bangladesh – which are already vulnerable to tropical storms – at even greater risk from storm surges and coastal flooding.

>> practice questions

1 **Explain how tropical storms are formed.**

2 **Describe the main features of a tropical storm.**

3 **How can people in LEDCs protect themselves from tropical storms?**

Drought

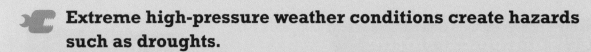
Extreme high-pressure weather conditions create hazards such as droughts.

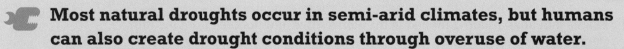
Most natural droughts occur in semi-arid climates, but humans can also create drought conditions through overuse of water.

A Causes of drought

remember >>

Most droughts happen in semi-arid regions.

① key fact A drought is when there is not enough rain over an extended period of time to support people or crops.

- Droughts develop in semi-arid climates in places experiencing anticyclone weather systems for long periods of time.

- These bring subtropical high pressure that holds water vapour and blows hot dry air outwards.

- The anticyclones also block depressions that bring moist air to the land.

② People can also induce drought conditions:

- by overuse of existing water supplies in homes, industry and agriculture

- by deforestation – cutting down trees reduces evapotranspiration, and therefore the amount of water vapour that can be released into the air. In turn, this limits clouds forming and rain falling.

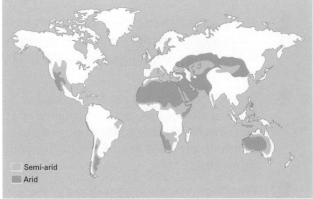
Semi-arid
Arid

B Effects of drought

The effects on land and people can be devastating when a fragile environment is mismanaged. In many cases there may be:

- overgrazing, which causes soil erosion and land degradation in arid and semi-arid areas – this is also called desertification

- crop failure, starvation of animals and water shortages, which cause famine and death

- increased migration from drought areas to towns and cities

- wildfires.

C Coping with drought

① key fact Short-term methods tend to be temporary and alleviate the impacts of a specific drought.

Common responses include water rationing and food and cash donations.

2 Long-term methods create permanent water management schemes. Dams, pipelines and irrigation systems will give more water for people to use every day. Although these methods will not help a drought which has already happened, they may prevent further droughts in the future and are therefore seen as sustainable.

remember >>

This topic links to water management on pages 124–5 and LEDC cities on pages 86–7.

D Case study – Droughts in the Sahel

1 **key fact** The Sahel region stretches from west to east across Africa. It is located just south of the Sahara desert between 12 and 17°N and includes some of the world's poorest countries. It often experiences drought.

The region includes countries such as Mali and Sudan. It is populated by nomads.

2 **key fact** For centuries the Sahel has fluctuated between periods of adequate rainfall and drought.

The most recent serious drought began in 2006 in Ethiopia. Drought happens when the wet air at the equator is stopped from moving northwards to the Sahel.

3 Continued hot dry air from the subtropical high-pressure zone over the region caused widespread land degradation.

4 The result was mass migration south of nomads and their livestock into the savannah.

5 **key fact** The increase in population, caused by the nomads' migration and high birth rates, put pressure on the fragile savannah ecosystem.

Trees were stripped for firewood, causing soil erosion. Now these areas are uninhabitable.

6 To avoid malnutrition and famine, the nomads have moved to cities such as Khartoum and Addis Ababa as refugees, causing urban problems.

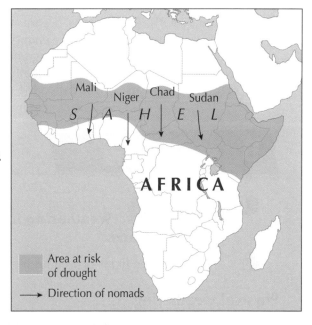

Mali Niger Chad Sudan

S A H E L

AFRICA

Area at risk of drought

→ Direction of nomads

>> practice questions

1 **What is a drought?**

2 **How do humans contribute to drought conditions?**

3 **Why is the Sahel prone to drought?**

4 **What are the impacts of drought on the nomads?**

exam tip >>

Make sure you learn a case study of an extreme weather event.

Rocks and weathering

- **There are three groups of rocks: igneous, sedimentary and metamorphic.**

- **Rocks can be broken down by the process of weathering.**

- **Weathering and erosion help shape the landscape and create distinct landforms.**

A Rock types

1 key fact The Earth is made up of many different types of rock. These are classified (organised) into three main groups.

Igneous rocks	These rocks are formed when **magma** from inside the Earth **cools** and **solidifies**. Examples of **igneous** rocks include **granite** and **basalt**.
Sedimentary rocks	These rocks are formed from **fragments** of other **rocks** or the **remains** of **living things** which have been **compressed into rocks**. Examples of **sedimentary** rocks include **sandstone, chalk** and **limestone**.
Metamorphic rocks	These are **existing** rocks that have been **changed** by **intense heat** and **pressure** to form **new rocks**. The new rocks are harder and more compact than the original rocks. Examples of how **metamorphic** rocks can form include **limestone** becoming **marble** or **sandstone** becoming **quartzite**.

2 However, the Earth's rocks do not stay the same forever. They are continually changing because of processes such as weathering and large earth movements. The rocks are gradually recycled over millions of years. This is called the rock cycle.

study hint >>

Make sure that you understand how each rock type forms, and be able to give an example of each type of rock.

B Weathering

1 key fact Weathering involves the breakdown of rocks on the Earth's surface.

2 There are three types of weathering: physical, chemical and biological.

Physical weathering

This is caused by changes in temperature or pressure. There are two main types of physical weathering:

- **Freeze-thaw weathering** takes place when water is trapped in the cracks of a rock and freezes. The frozen water expands and enlarges the cracks. The process of freeze-thaw weathering repeats until the rock is weakened and shatters.

Cracks fill with water

Water freezes and expands as ice. It then thaws.

Cracks widen, pieces of rock split off

- **Onion-skin weathering** takes place in hot desert climates. During the heat of the day, the surface of the rock heats up and expands. At night it is cold and the rock contracts. This causes thin layers of rock to peel off.

Heat causes outer layer of rock to expand

Cold nights cause outer layer to contract

Outer layer flakes off

Chemical weathering

Chemical weathering occurs when weak acids in rainwater attack and break down the minerals in the rocks (carbonation). Some materials are dissolved and carried away from the weathering source and deposited as sediments, which eventually become compacted to form sedimentary rocks. Thus chemical weathering plays a part in the rock cycle. Limestone is weathered in this way.

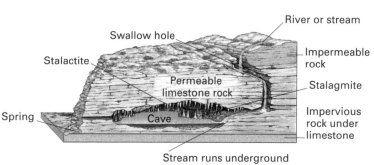

Biological weathering

This involves plants and animals. Plant seeds can begin to grow in the cracks of a rock. As the roots expand, the cracks in the rock expand, the rock weakens and pieces break off.

3 Once rocks have been broken down they may be eroded or transported.

Erosion is the wearing away of the land by water, ice or wind.

C Different landscapes

1 **key fact** The study of rocks and different rock types is called geology. The geology of an area is a key factor influencing the shape of the landscape.

2 Stronger rocks tend to produce highland areas whereas weaker rocks tend to form lowland areas. Whether rocks allow water to pass through them tells you whether they are permeable or impermeable. Water will pass through permeable rocks. Water is not able to pass through impermeable rocks. The permeability of rocks will determine how wet or dry the surface of a landscape is.

3 Limestone (karst) is a permeable rock that tends to form dry upland areas with few streams and thin soils.

4 Clay is an impermeable rock that tends to produce wet lowland areas.

5 Rocks are also used as a resource by humans, who quarry stone for use in construction, as aquifers for water supply and as unique scenery for tourism. This has both advantages and disadvantages.

>> practice questions

1 **What is the difference between erosion and weathering?**

2 **How is igneous rock formed?**

3 **Describe how chemical weathering shapes limestone scenery.**

Glaciation

- During the Ice Age, many areas across the world, including the UK, were permanently covered by ice.

- A glacier is a body of ice that moves through a valley.

- Glaciers have shaped many landscapes through the processes of erosion, transportation and deposition.

A   The Ice Age

remember >>
Glaciers are still shaping parts of the world today.

① key fact   Many landscapes across the world, including parts of the UK, have been shaped by ice.

② During the last Ice Age, which lasted from 2 million to 10 000 years ago (the Pleistocene), the climate was much colder than it is today.

③ In upland areas, snow remained on the ground all year. As more and more snow was added each year, it slowly compressed to form ice.

④ In some areas, enormous ice sheets covered the whole landscape. During the Ice Age, the whole of northern Britain was covered in ice. In other places, ice only filled the valleys, forming glaciers. Over time, these glaciers moved downhill and shaped the landscape in many parts of Britain.

⑤ Today, ice and snow still permanently cover countries within the Arctic Circle, such as Greenland, northern Canada and parts of Russia. Glaciers are found in highland areas such as the Himalayas and the Alps.

B   Glacial erosion

① Glaciers form in hollows (corries) on the colder, sheltered side of a mountain.

- Snow and ice gather in the hollow and, over time, the corrie gets larger through freeze-thaw weathering (see page 26).

- Inside the hollow, the ice begins to move in a circular motion, called rotational slip.

- Eventually, the ice will move out of the corrie and over the lip of the hollow.

② As a glacier moves down the mountainside, it erodes the landscape in two main ways:

Franz Josef Glacier, New Zealand

- **Plucking**: this occurs when meltwater under a glacier freezes onto the rock surface. As the glacier moves forward, it pulls away large fragments of rock from the rock surface.

- **Abrasion**: this occurs when pieces of rock carried by the ice wear away the landscape, like sandpaper.

③ Other erosional features occur in upland areas. An arête is a steep knife-edged ridge between two corries. A tarn is a meltwater lake left behind in a corrie.

C Glacial deposition

1 As a glacier moves downhill, temperatures rise and the glacier begins to melt.

2 As the glacier melts, it deposits the material it has been carrying.

3 This deposition usually takes place in lowland areas.

4 **key fact** Glacial deposition creates a number of distinct landscape features in lowland areas.

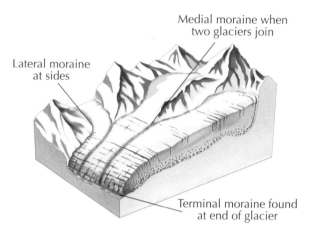

Lateral moraine at sides

Medial moraine when two glaciers join

Terminal moraine found at end of glacier

- **Moraine** is the rock material carried by the glacier. It is later deposited to form mounds of unsorted rocks and rock particles, which are called moraines. There are several different types of moraine. They are classified according to when and where they were deposited by the glacier.

- **Drumlins** are mounds of boulder clay, deposited by glaciers and shaped by the moving ice. The ice moved over the drumlins to form small egg-shaped hills.

- **Erratics** are rocks transported many miles by a glacier and later found in an area of a different rock type.

D Glaciation and recreation

1 **key fact** Glaciation helped to create distinctive and interesting landscapes (e.g. the Lake District). These glacial landforms provide an important resource for the tourist industry.

- Tourists and day visitors may visit these areas to go walking, hiking, skiing, mountaineering or abseiling.

- Many glaciated landscapes are managed and protected from large-scale urban or industrial development. Many are National Park areas where the main land use is primary industry.

- This creates conflict and issues over the use of such areas for recreation (see pages 110–11).

>> practice questions

1 Using geographical terms, explain how a glacier erodes the landscape.

2 For a named glaciated environment that you have studied, describe how the land is used and explain why conflict may occur between the different groups of people using that landscape.

The river system

Systems are important in geography.

The river system is part of the hydrological system (the water cycle).

Water falling around a river may reach the river channel in a number of different ways.

A Systems in geography

1. Systems are an important part of geography. For example, you may have studied ecological systems, farming systems or industrial systems.

2. Geographical systems can be open or closed.

   • An open system has inputs and outputs.

   • A closed system has no inputs or outputs; it is a continuous cycle.

3. A river is an open system with inputs, processes and outputs.

4. **key fact** The river system is part of larger system called the hydrological cycle.

B The hydrological cycle

1. The hydrological cycle is a closed system. Water is continuously transferred from the world's oceans into the atmosphere and then onto land, before returning back into the oceans.

2. Water moves through the hydrological cycle through a series of flows, or transfers. Water is also stored within the system (e.g. in a lake).

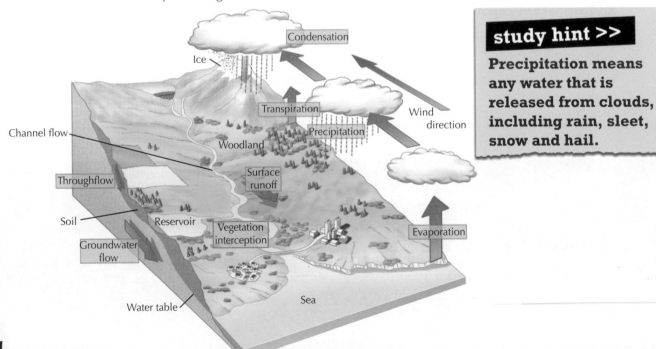

study hint >>

Precipitation means any water that is released from clouds, including rain, sleet, snow and hail.

C The river system

1 **key fact** The river system is an open system, with inputs, processes, stores and outputs.

2 The source is where a river begins its journey. The mouth is where the river reaches the end of its journey.

3 The area of land drained by a river and its tributaries is called the drainage basin (sometimes called a catchment area).

4 Tributaries are the small rivers that join the main river channel. The point at which two rivers meet is called a confluence. The greater the number of tributaries, the denser the drainage basin.

5 The boundary between two drainage basins is known as the watershed. A watershed is usually a ridge of highland.

6 Water falling to the ground can travel to a river in many ways (some of these flows and transfers are similar to those found in the hydrological cycle):

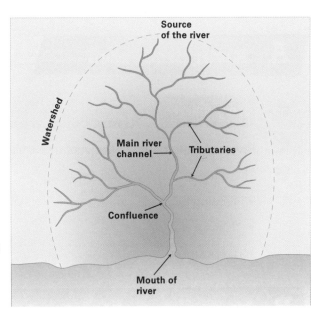

- Water may infiltrate into the soil layer and move slowly towards the river. This is called throughflow (or soil flow).

- Water may percolate through the soil to the rock layer below. Water moving through the rocks towards the river is called groundwater flow or base flow.

- Some water flows directly over the ground to the river. This is called overland flow or surface runoff.

- Some water does not reach the river channel; it may be intercepted or stored. Water may be intercepted by vegetation. It can be stored at surface level (e.g. in a glacier) or below ground (e.g. in the soil or rock layer).

>> practice questions

1 Explain what is meant by the following terms:

a) drainage basin
b) watershed
c) tributary
d) confluence.

2 Describe two ways in which water may reach a river channel.

3 Explain how water may be stored in the river system.

River processes

- A river contains energy. It uses this energy to carry out river processes.

- There are three main river processes: erosion, transportation and deposition.

- The journey of a river from source to mouth is called the long profile.

A   River processes

1 **key fact** Rivers contain energy.

2 Rivers use their energy to overcome friction and carry out river processes.

3 There are three main river processes:

- Erosion
- Transportation
- Deposition.

B   The long profile of a river

1 A river changes as it travels from the source to the mouth.

2 The course of a river can be divided into three main sections: the upper course, middle course and lower course.

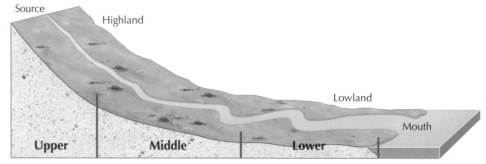

Source

Highland

Lowland

Mouth

Upper   Middle   Lower

3 Rivers begin flowing in highland areas and flow downwards to lowland areas.

C   Erosion

1 Rivers can erode in four ways:

- **Hydraulic action:** The force of the water wears away the bed and banks of the river.

- **Abrasion (or corrasion):** Rocks and pebbles being carried by the river wear away the bed and banks of the river.

- **Attrition:** Rocks and pebbles being carried by the river knock together and are broken down into smaller particles.

study hint >>

Some of the methods of river erosion sound similar. Each is different, so learn them carefully.

- **Solution (or corrosion):** Weak acids in the water dissolve rocks and minerals in the river channel. Chalk and limestone are two rock types that dissolve relatively easily.

2️⃣ Erosion can be vertical or lateral.

- **Vertical** (downward) erosion takes place in the upper course of the river, as gravity pulls the water downwards. Vertical erosion deepens the river channel and can create V-shaped valleys.

- **Lateral** (sideways) erosion takes place in the middle and lower courses of the river. Lateral erosion widens the river channel.

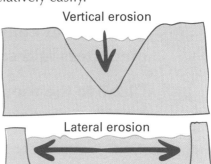

Vertical erosion

Lateral erosion

D Transportation

Rivers can use their energy to transport material.

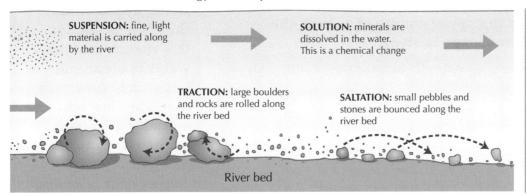

SUSPENSION: fine, light material is carried along by the river

SOLUTION: minerals are dissolved in the water. This is a chemical change

TRACTION: large boulders and rocks are rolled along the river bed

SALTATION: small pebbles and stones are bounced along the river bed

River bed

remember >>

The size of the material being carried by the river will affect the way it is transported.

E Deposition

1️⃣ **key fact** If a river loses energy and slows down, it deposits (drops) the load that it has been carrying.

2️⃣ A river may lose energy if:

- it enters an area of shallow water

- it enters an area of vegetation

- the volume (amount) of water in the river decreases, e.g. after a flood.

3️⃣ Most deposition takes place in the lower course of the river. The smallest material is dropped first.

remember >>

Rivers are also affected by weathering. See pages 48–9 on weathering.

>> practice questions

1 **Describe the different ways in which a river may carry out erosion.**

2 **Explain how a river may transport natural material.**

River landscapes and features

- In the upper course of the river, vertical erosion can create V-shaped valleys and interlocking spurs.

- In the lower course of the river, lateral erosion can help to create meanders and sometimes oxbow lakes.

- Close to the mouth of the river, a wide floodplain, and sometimes a delta, is created.

A Features in the upper course of a river

1 **key fact** In the upper course of a river, the gradient of the landscape is steep.

2 At its source, a river erodes vertically (downwards), cutting into the landscape to form a steep-sided V-shaped valley.

3 In the upper course of the river, the channel is narrow and the river erodes its way through areas of softer rock. As the river cuts through the softer rock, it winds to avoid areas of hard rock. This can lead to the formation of interlocking spurs.

4 Rapids may also form in the upper course of the river, when the river travels over alternating bands of hard and soft rock.

5 Waterfalls are a common feature in the upper course of many larger rivers. A waterfall occurs when a layer of hard, resistant rock, lies over a layer of softer rock that will erode more easily.

remember >>

In the upper course, the river is young; this means that the water is clear and appears to flow very fast. The flow will actually get faster as the river moves downstream and more water is added to the channel.

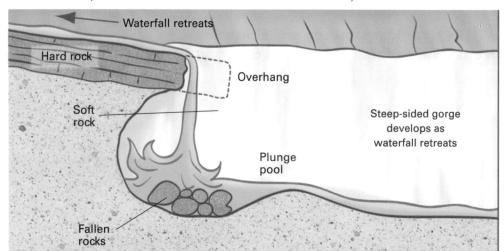

Labels: Waterfall retreats; Hard rock; Overhang; Soft rock; Steep-sided gorge develops as waterfall retreats; Plunge pool; Fallen rocks

B Features in the middle and lower courses of a river

1 **key fact** In the lower course of the river, the gradient is gentler than in the upper course. The river has more energy and the volume of water is high.

2 In the lower course of the river, there is more lateral (sideways) erosion. The channel is wide and deep. The river has less friction to overcome, which means it can flow faster.

3 As the river erodes sideways, it swings from side to side, forming large bends called meanders.

4 Over time, the loop of a meander becomes tighter. If it becomes too tight, the river may simply cut across the neck of the meander to form a straight river channel. The loop is cut off from the main channel and forms an oxbow lake.

study hint >>

Remember, the features found in and around a river are strongly influenced by the geology of the area (the types of rock found there).

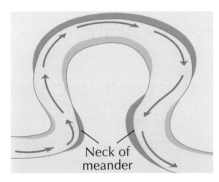

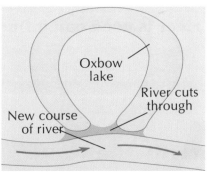

Oxbow lake

River cuts through

New course of river

Neck of meander

■ Erosion   ■ Deposition

→ Fastest flow

C Features at the mouth of a river

1 **key fact** As the river reaches the mouth, it has a large discharge and the river channel is deep and wide. The velocity of the water has also increased.

2 The river valley is now wide and flat. This creates a wide floodplain around the river.

3 A floodplain is a flat area around a river that regularly floods. Each time a river floods, silt (alluvium) is deposited on the floodplain. This makes the floodplain very fertile, which is good for farming and agriculture. Floodplains are often highly populated, particularly in LEDCs (Less Economically Developed Countries), where farming employs many people.

4 Deltas are a feature found in at the mouth of many large rivers (e.g. the Ganges Delta). They are created through an accumulation of deposited silt. Deltas are rich in alluvium and provide fertile farmland.

There are three main types of delta:

- **Arcuate**, e.g. The Nile Delta, Egypt – this is shaped like a fan

- **Cuspate**, e.g. The Ebro Delta, Spain – this is evenly shaped

- **Birds foot**, e.g. The Mississippi Delta, USA – the distributaries are spread out like a bird's claw.

>> practice questions

1 List some of the features found in the upper course of a river.

2 Using a simple diagram, explain how an oxbow lake is formed.

3 With reference to named examples, explain why people often live in high densities (high numbers) in the lower course of a river.

Flooding and hydrographs

- River discharge is the amount of water passing through a river at a given point.

- Hydrographs are used to show changes in river discharge over time.

- A significant rise in river discharge could lead to flooding.

- How the land around a river is used can influence how likely it is to flood.

A River discharge

1. River discharge is measured in cumecs (cubic metres per second).

2. The discharge of a river varies over time. A sudden increase in discharge may cause a flood.

3. Human and physical factors will influence river discharge:

The weather	Geology	Land use	Engineering
A period of heavy rain will increase river discharge. A period of drought will lower river discharge.	The rocks found in and around the channel of a river may influence river discharge. For example, in an area of permeable rock, the discharge of the river may be less than in an area of impermeable rock.	The way in which land around a river is used can increase or decrease the chances of flooding; for example, building on a floodplain increases the impermeability of the land and raises the flood risk.	Humans can engineer or change the natural course of a river. Depending upon what changes are made to the river, the discharge may increase or decrease.

B Flooding

1. **key fact** A flood occurs when a river overflows its banks and water spreads onto the surrounding land. Some rivers flood regularly and others rarely flood.

2. **key fact** The faster the water reaches a river, the more likely it is to flood.

✖ Floods can be devastating, claiming lives and destroying homes.

✔ Floods can benefit people and the environment. For example, when a river floods, it deposits fine silt and sediment which help to fertilise the soil, generating excellent conditions for farming. People living near rivers such as the Nile in Egypt rely on regular flooding.

✖ Floods tend to have a worse impact on LEDCs than they do on MEDCs. An example of an LEDC that suffers from regular flooding is Bangladesh. LEDCs do not have enough equipment to accurately predict floods. Poor communications can make evacuation difficult, and LEDCs lack the resources needed to rebuild their country once the flood waters subside.

3 The landscape influences how fast water reaches the main river channel.

- In wooded areas, trees may intercept precipitation. Trees collect rainwater on their leaves; some water is taken up by their roots.

- In rural areas, fields that have crops growing in them will intercept rainfall. However, if a field is left bare and the soil becomes dry, the water will not permeate into the soil and will travel overland to the river.

- Steep slopes in highland areas cause water to flow quickly down the slopes towards the river (overland flow).

- In urban areas, the landscape is made up mainly of impermeable rock (concrete). This means that water travels quickly towards the river by overland flow. Drains also take water directly to the river channel. Many houses in urban areas have sloping roofs, which also increases runoff.

C Hydrographs

1 Changes in river discharge over time are shown using a hydrograph.

2 A hydrograph shows two variables: rainfall (shown using bars) and river discharge (shown using a line).

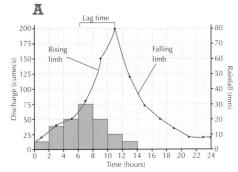

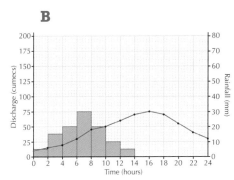

3 The difference between the peak (highest) rainfall and the peak discharge is called the lag time.

4 The longer the lag time, the less chance there is of a river flooding. A short lag time means that the water has reached the river channel quickly and there is a higher risk of flooding.

5 The base flow on a hydrograph shows the volume of water reaching a river through groundwater flow.

6 The rising limb shows the increase in river discharge, while the falling limb shows the decrease in river discharge.

>> practice questions

1 **Explain two ways in which human activity can increase the risk of flooding.**

2 **At what time was the peak discharge on graph B?**

3 **Which graph, A or B, appears to show river discharge patterns for an urban area? Explain your answer.**

Managing flooding

- People often try to manage rivers to reduce the risk of flooding.

- Flood management can involve hard engineering schemes or soft engineering schemes.

- Flood management has advantages and disadvantages for people and the environment.

A Flood management

1 **key fact** The risk of flooding and the impact of flooding can be reduced in a variety of ways.

2 Controlling flooding can involve using hard or soft engineering:

- Hard engineering options tend to involve making significant changes to the natural river channel. These changes tend to be costly and long-lasting.

- Soft engineering options tend to be low-cost and do not involve making significant changes to the natural river channel.

3 Flood management and prediction tend to be more effective and accurate in MEDCs. LEDCs often lack the resources needed for effective flood management.

> **remember >>**
> Each method of flood management has costs and benefits.

B Hard engineering options

1 **key fact** Hard engineering options tend to be costly and have a significant impact upon the natural environment.

2 **Building a dam:** Constructing a dam in the upper course of a river allows people to control the amount of discharge in the river further downstream.

✔	Water is held back behind the dam and it can be released in controlled amounts.
✔	The water held behind the dam is usually stored in a reservoir. The water in the reservoir can then be used to help generate power (hydroelectric power) or for leisure and recreation, e.g. water sports.
✘	Building dams is expensive and can spoil the look of the natural environment.
✘	Building a dam can mean that sediment is trapped in the upper sections of the river, which can cause coastal erosion at the mouth of the river.
✘	As the river is no longer able to flood naturally, the fertility of the floodplain may be reduced. This can affect agriculture, particularly in LEDCs.

3 **Modifying the river channel:** The river can be made straighter and deeper, which allows more water to flow quickly through the channel. This can reduce the risk of flooding in some areas. However, it can increase the risk of flooding further downstream, and wetland habitats may be harmed or destroyed.

C Soft engineering options

1 | **key fact** | Soft engineering options tend to be low-cost and do not have a significant impact upon the natural environment. Soft options are also cheaper and easier to maintain than hard engineering options.

2 Some argue that soft engineering is more sustainable than hard engineering.

3 **Afforestation:** This involves planting trees and vegetation around the river channel, helping to lower river discharge and therefore reducing the risk of flooding. The leaves of trees and roots of trees intercept rainwater and reduce runoff.

4 **Ecological flooding:** Some parts of the river are allowed to flood naturally in rural areas, to prevent flooding in urban areas.

5 **Landuse planning:** Governments and local authorities can prevent or limit the number of homes constructed close to or in flood-risk areas.

6 **Preparation:** People in flood-risk areas can be educated about how to prepare for flooding.

D Case study – The River Valency, Boscastle, Cornwall

1 The river Valency flows through the coastal village of Boscastle to the sea.

2 The river flooded in August 2004, causing extensive damage (buildings were damaged and many vehicles were washed away from the village car park).

3 Since 2004, various river management schemes have been put into place. These include a mixture of hard and soft engineering:

- Floodwalls, or retaining walls, have been built along sections of the riverbanks.

- The old bridge which crossed the river has been removed and replaced with a modern one. During the flood, debris got trapped behind the old bridge, causing a dangerous build-up of water. The new bridge is higher and wider.

- In places, the river has been widened and deepened.

- The village car park has been raised to higher ground so that cars would not be washed away in another flood. Hedges have been planted to divide the car park into sections.

4 In 2007, Boscastle experienced more flooding, but the impact was minor compared with the 2004 flood.

>> practice questions

1 **Using examples, describe how people can try to control river flooding. (Hint: remember to talk about hard and soft engineering in your answer.)**

2 **For a named flood management scheme that you have studied, explain the costs and the benefits of the scheme for people and the environment.**

Wave power

- The coast is a fragile environment and is constantly changing as a result of marine and aerial processes.

- Wave power influences the landforms that are found along the coastline.

A Wave energy

remember >>

The power of the waves depends on wind and the fetch, and these determine the processes that take place.

① key fact Waves are made when wind blows over the surface of the sea, creating friction.

② Friction with the seabed slows down the bottom of the wave but the top of the wave continues moving at the same rate and topples forward, breaking against a cliff or beach when it becomes unstable.

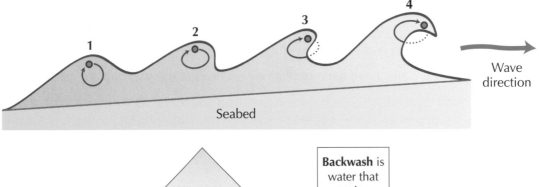

Water particles move in circular pattern

Friction with seabed increases as water becomes shallow. Pattern becomes egg-shaped

Top of wave not affected by friction

Wave becomes steeper and breaks up the beach

Seabed

Wave direction

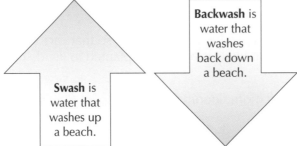

Swash is water that washes up a beach.

Backwash is water that washes back down a beach.

③ key fact The size and energy of a wave are greatest when the wind is strong, has been blowing for a long time and has come a long way.

④ key fact The distance a wave has travelled over is called the fetch.

B Types of wave

1 key fact The type of wave determines the shape of the beach.

2 key fact There are two types of wave: constructive and destructive.

Constructive waves are longer and flatter, happen in calm conditions (usually summer) and have strong swash which transports material up the beach. They create shallow beaches by depositing material.

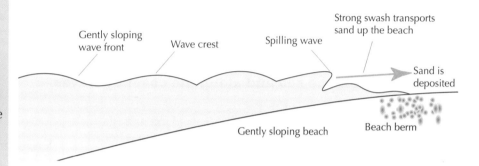

Gently sloping wave front
Wave crest
Spilling wave
Strong swash transports sand up the beach
Sand is deposited
Gently sloping beach
Beach berm

Destructive waves are taller and shorter in length, happen more in stormy weather (usually winter) and have strong backwash which erodes material from the beach. They create beaches by eroding material.

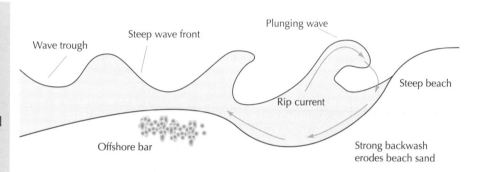

Wave trough
Steep wave front
Plunging wave
Steep beach
Rip current
Offshore bar
Strong backwash erodes beach sand

exam tip >>
Make sure you can draw your own version of these diagrams.

>> practice questions

1 **What causes waves?**

2 **Which factors control the amount of energy a wave has?**

3 **Explain the term 'fetch'.**

4 **Explain the difference between constructive and destructive waves.**

Coastal processes

> There are three main processes at work in the sea: transportation, erosion and deposition.

> The impact of these processes is dependent on the rock type and structure present at the coastline.

A Transportation

remember >>

Longshore drift moves material along a beach.

① **key fact** Transportation is the movement of material in the sea and along the coast by waves.

Solution: dissolved salt and calcium carbonate in the water

Suspension: sand and silt carried in the water

Traction: boulders rolled along the seabed by strong wave action

Transport by the sea

Saltation: pebbles bounced along the seabed by wave action

② Transport along the coast is when waves move material across a beach. This is called longshore drift. It happens when:

- The prevailing wind causes the waves to break on the beach at an angle.

- Swash carries the material up the beach at an angle.

- Backwash drags the material back down the beach at right angles.

- Each wave pushes material further along the beach.

- Material is moved along the beach in the direction of the prevailing wind.

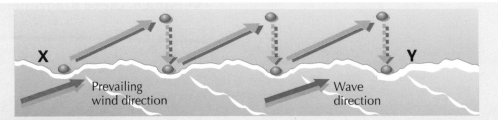

X

Y

Prevailing wind direction

Wave direction

B Erosion

① **key fact** Erosion is caused by destructive waves wearing away the coastline. It happens when the waves are packed with energy. Erosion destroys landforms.

2 Waves erode rocks in three ways:

- **Hydraulic action** is when waves crash against cliffs, trapping and compressing air and water in rock cracks. As the waves move back, pressure is released, causing the air and water to expand. This explodes, breaking off rock fragments.

- **Abrasion** is when breaking waves pound rocks and pebbles against the cliffs, wearing the land away in a sandpaper effect.

- **Attrition** is when waves smash rock fragments against each other, making pebbles smoother, rounder and smaller. After a time, the particles are ground into grit and sand.

3 The rate of erosion of any coastal landform depends on the following:

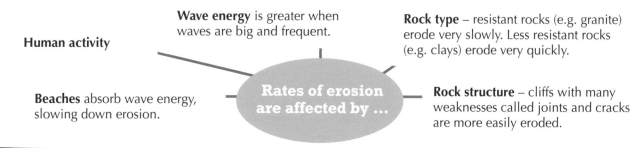

Wave energy is greater when waves are big and frequent.

Human activity

Rock type – resistant rocks (e.g. granite) erode very slowly. Less resistant rocks (e.g. clays) erode very quickly.

Beaches absorb wave energy, slowing down erosion.

Rates of erosion are affected by ...

Rock structure – cliffs with many weaknesses called joints and cracks are more easily eroded.

C Deposition

>> key fact **Deposition is the dumping of eroded material along the coast.**

Deposition happens when the waves lose power and no longer have the energy to transport the material they are carrying.

D Weathering and mass movement

1 Sub-aerial weathering can occur along the top and at the face of a cliff.

2 **key fact** **Sub-aerial weathering can speed up rates of cliff erosion.**

3 This can happen chemically and physically (see pages 48–9).

4 Mass movements can also occur along the coast. A mass movement is the slide downslope of rock and soil due to gravity.

5 Rockfalls, mudslides and landslides may occur when the material that makes up the cliff is weakened or becomes unstable due to erosion and/or weathering.

>> practice questions

1 **Using the longshore drift diagram, explain how material may be moved between points X and Y.**

2 **When is deposition most likely to happen?**

3 **What is the role of geology in erosion?**

4 **How does rock type affect weathering and mass movement?**

Landforms created by erosion

- The interaction of the processes of transport, erosion and deposition creates coastal landforms.

- These processes may be made faster or slower by geology, weathering and humans.

A Cliffs and wave-cut platforms

>> **key fact** A cliff made from soft rock will erode quickly and form a gently sloping cliff. Hard rock creates steep cliffs.

A wave-cut platform may be created in front of a cliff.

1 Hydraulic action, abrasion and corrosion attack the coastline between the high- and low-water marks. This creates a notch at the base of the cliff and an overhang above.

2 The cliff above collapses.

3 Over time, the collapsed material erodes to form beach material and the cliff retreats, leaving a wave-cut platform in front of the cliff; for example, at Southerndown, South Wales).

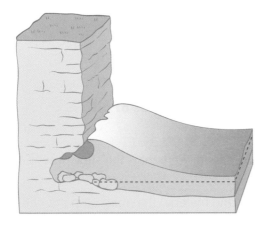 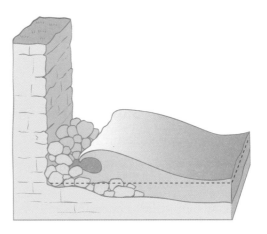

B Headlands and bays

>> **key fact** Headlands and bays form when alternating bands of hard and soft rock are found along a stretch of coastline.

exam tip >>

If you are asked to explain how coastal features are formed, draw labelled diagrams as part of your answer.

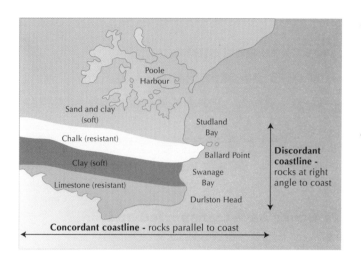

- Destructive waves erode the softer rock faster than the hard, resistant rock. The softer rock is worn away to form a bay (e.g. Swanage Bay), whilst the resistant rock is left exposed, jutting out into the sea to form a headland (e.g. Ballard Point).

- When rocks are found at a right angle to the sea, it is called a discordant coastline.

Étretat, Normandy, France

C Caves, arches and stacks

>> **key fact** Caves, arches, stacks and stumps are made when a narrow headland made from hard rock is eroded.

Strong waves attack cracks and weaknesses in the rock by hydraulic action, abrasion and corrosion to make **caves**. (The cave may develop a blow hole if hydraulic action happens along a weakness in the cave roof, causing collapse.)

Arches form as the caves erode even more and break through the headland.

Stacks form when the roof of the arch collapses.

Stumps, which are only seen at low tide, are left behind once the stack has eroded.

>> practice questions

1 In which feature would you find a notch?

2 With which rock types are headlands associated?

3 Look at the diagram. Name features A, B, C and D. Now explain how D is formed.

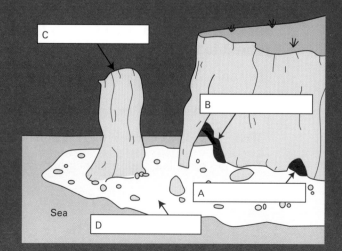

Depositional landforms

 Coastal processes can create depositional landforms.

 Two main landforms are created: beaches and spits.

A Beaches

>> **key fact** **Beaches are found where waves have transported and deposited eroded material from the sea.**

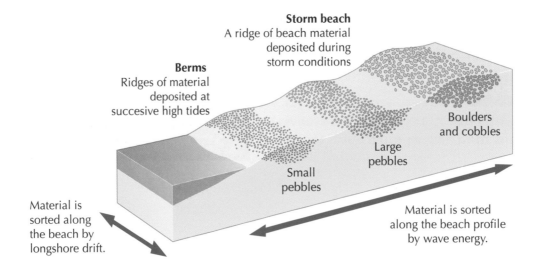

Storm beach
A ridge of beach material deposited during storm conditions

Berms
Ridges of material deposited at succesive high tides

Boulders and cobbles

Large pebbles

Small pebbles

Material is sorted along the beach by longshore drift.

Material is sorted along the beach profile by wave energy.

- Beaches can be found on wave-cut platforms or in bays. Whether the beach is sand or pebble will depend on rock type and wave energy, as will the size and height of the beach.

- The beach profile above shows that the largest material is deposited on the storm beach closest to the cliff during storms. Below this are berms. These are ridges of material dumped at high tide. The smallest material is deposited closest to the shoreline.

B Spits

>> **key fact** **Spits are extended beaches of pebbles or sand that are joined to the land at one end and stretch out into the sea at the other end.**

They only form when certain conditions are present:

The sea is shallow and the current is weak, to allow deposition.
There is a sudden change in the direction of the coastline or a river mouth.
There is a prevailing wind and longshore drift.

Step 1: Longshore drift moves material beyond the change in coastline.

Step 2: The spit is formed when the material is deposited.

Step 3: Over time, the spit grows in length and may develop a hook if wind direction changes further out.

Step 4: Waves cannot get behind the spit, creating a sheltered area where silt is deposited and mud flats or salt marshes form.

study hint >>

You might be asked about two other depositional landforms, such as bars and tombolos; these are also linked to the process of longshore drift, so research these as well.

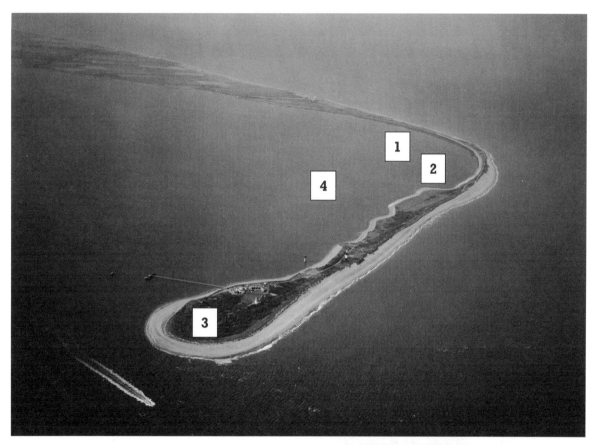

Spurn Head, Humberside

exam tip >>

Put the diagrams you draw in the exam into a frame.

>> practice questions

1 How are beaches made?

2 Draw a sketch of Spurn Head spit in the photograph above.

3 Label your sketch to explain how the spit has formed.

4 Why are spits often used for leisure and tourism activities?

Managing the coastline

- As coastal settlements grow in size, more people are at risk from coastal flooding.

- The risk of coastal flooding is increasing as climate change leads to a rise in sea-level and more frequent storm events.

- There are conflicts between managing coasts to meet the needs of different groups of people, to balance the costs and benefits and to protect the environment.

A Why protect coastlines?

1. **key fact** Many coastlines in MEDCs are heavily populated and have high economic value.

2. Coasts provide people with income in the tourism and leisure industries.

3. Many coastlines are prone to flooding or erosion.

4. Many coastlines are fragile, natural environments, which are easily damaged by people. If they are destroyed, ecosystems take a long time to recover.

B Managing the coast

1. **key fact** For most stretches of coastline in the UK there is a shoreline management plan (SMP) which sets out how the coastline should be managed.

2. Local councils can use four strategies when deciding how to manage the coast:

   - **Do nothing** – let nature take its course so the coastline is abandoned.

   - **Managed retreat/alignment** – a decision is made to let the coast erode/flood naturally with monitoring and to compensate those affected.

   - **Hold the line** – protect the current coastline using sea defences.

   - **Advance the line** – reclaim land from the sea and build new defences seaward.

3. In deciding what action to take, several factors are taken into consideration:

   - the economic costs and benefits of coastal management strategies

   - the needs of people in the area

   - the surrounding environment.

4. The government and local councils are keen to develop coastal management plans that are sustainable (costs are kept low and natural processes are not greatly altered). However, this is not always possible.

C Coastal management techniques

Hard and soft engineering methods are used to defend coastlines against erosion and flooding.

- **Hard engineering** techniques are expensive in terms of building costs and maintenance. They can be ugly and are often unsustainable as they battle against natural processes, sometimes causing damage in other places down the coast.

Groynes	Wooden/rock barriers at right angles to the beach. Beach material builds up against it, creating a wider beach that absorbs wave energy. Groynes are used along coasts with longshore drift.
Sea walls	Concrete barriers built at the base of cliffs or to protect a settlement behind from erosion or flooding. They work by deflecting the waves. Sometimes this wave energy depletes the beach. Sometimes they are curved.
Revetments	Wooden/concrete slatted barriers built towards the back of the beach to protect a cliff base or sea wall. Waves break against the revetments, which dissipate the energy.
Rip-rap/rock armour	Large rocks are piled up the back of the beach to protect a cliff base or sea wall from erosion. It works by absorbing wave energy.
Gabions	Boulders and rocks are wired into mesh cages and placed in front of cliffs and sea walls. Wave energy is absorbed by the rocks, limiting erosion.

- **Soft engineering** techniques work with nature and tend to have lower maintenance costs. They are usually sustainable as they work with natural processes, causing little damage.

Cliff stabilisation	By draining off excess rainwater in pipes, waterlogging is reduced in cliffs prone to slumping. Cliffs may also be wired and vegetation planted on the cliff face to make them more stable.
Beach nourishment	Increases beach size by replacing beach material lost through longshore drift with material dredged from the seabed and pumped onto the beach. It works by absorbing wave energy, which slows erosion and provides a flood barrier.
Stabilising sand dunes	By planting grasses to hold dunes in place and introducing footpaths to reduce trampling, the rate of erosion is slowed and an effective flood barrier is created.

>> practice questions

1 Who is responsible for most sea defences in the UK?
2 What is the difference between hard and soft engineering?
3 Choose two hard engineering methods. What are their advantages and disadvantages?

Coastal case studies

- The village of Happisburgh is being badly affected by erosion.

- Some steps have been taken to manage this problem.

- Porlock Bay experiences coastal flooding.

- The Shoreline Management Plan is allowing part of the area to revert back to being a lagoon – this is sustainable coastal management.

Case study 1 – Managing erosion in Happisburgh, Norfolk

1. Happisburgh is a small village on the north Norfolk Coast.

2. This Norfolk coastline suffers a great deal from erosion by the North Sea.

   - The cliffs are attacked at the top by heavy rain (sub-aerial weathering) and at the base (bottom) by waves.

   - The sands and clay cliffs are not very resistant to erosion. This means the cliffs retreat (move back).

   - Also, millions of tonnes of sand have been dredged from the seabed. This affects the beach, which is a natural barrier to erosion.

3. The Shoreline Management Plan (SMP) for Norfolk states that Happisburgh will not be protected from coastal erosion in future years.

   - This document was written by DEFRA (the Department of Environment, Food and Rural Affairs).

   - DEFRA argues that it is not economically viable to protect Happisburgh in the future.

4. Happisburgh has some coastal defences: revetments and groynes. These are broken and in need of repair. DEFRA has said that they will not be repaired or replaced.

5. Erosion has had an impact on the village. In 2002, a 30-metre stretch of the coastline was lost to the sea in a large storm.

   - The village tea shop and guest house has had to move to a new location away from the retreating cliff. Sometimes it has been forced to close because there is not enough business to keep it open.

   - The erosion has reduced property prices in the area.

6. Over 2500 people have petitioned against the shoreline management plan for this area.

   - A local action group, Coastal Concern Action Group (CCAG), has been set up to try to protect the village against erosion.

   - In 2007, 4000 tonnes of rock armour was put on the beach at Happisburgh. The scheme was funded by North Norfolk District Council as well as local villagers and international supporters.

   - It is predicted that over the next five years the cliffs will retreat by 30–75 m.

Happisburgh beach defences

study hint >>

Find out more about the Shoreline Management Plan on the Internet.

Case study 2 – Managed retreat in Porlock Bay, West Somerset

1 Porlock Bay is a 4 km stretch of Exmoor's 55 km coastline. The bay has two headlands: Gore Point to the west and Hurlstone Point to the east.

Porlock Bay is covered by the Bridgwater Bay to Bideford Bay Shoreline Management Plan.

2 The bay is sheltered by high moorland. The land immediately behind the bay is used for farming. Some of this land is a freshwater marsh.

3 Along the beach at Porlock Bay there is a large shingle ridge. This is at least 6000 years old and was formed with the rise in sea levels at the end of the last Ice Age.

4 A problem in recent years has been the weakening of the shingle ridge that protects Porlock Marsh, which is a Site of Special Scientific Interest.

- In the past, the ridge was topped up by fallen rock from the cliff at Gore Point. This natural supply of rock material no longer reaches the beach as there is a groyne at Porlock Weir. This stops the transportation of material eastwards by longshore drift. The material on the shingle ridge is constantly being transported away by the sea to build up the beach at Hurlstone Point. This weakens the ridge.

- The shingle ridge has also been weakened by high water levels and stormy weather. A storm in October 1996 breached the beach, leaving a permanent gap in the ridge. This means that the farmland and marsh behind are now flooded at high spring tides and a salt marsh is developing.

5 After major storms, the shingle ridge used to be rebuilt by filling in the gaps with new shingle. New breakwaters were also built to protect the farmland and freshwater marsh behind the ridge.

Predictions suggest that the sea level in this area will rise by between 20 cm and 70 cm in the next 50 years due to global warming. There is also likely to be an increase in very severe gales and coastal flooding.

6 After consultation with the National Trust, who own part of the ridge, Exmoor National Park Authority, English Nature and environmental consultants, a policy of 'managed retreat' has been implemented (see page 48). This could mean that in the future Porlock Marsh will once again become a lagoon, as it was 200 years ago.

Overlooking Porlock Bay

>> practice questions

1 **What are the causes of erosion along the coast off Happisburgh?**

2 **How have people tried to manage erosion in Happisburgh?**

3 **Describe the impact of coastal flooding in Porlock Bay.**

4 **Why is using managed retreat in Porlock Bay the most sustainable approach?**

5 **Who might object to this approach and why?**

Weather and climate

- The weather is the daily conditions in an area. Climate is weather patterns over a long time.

- The angle of the sun and rotation of the Earth are the main factors affecting world climate patterns.

A Weather and climate

① key fact Weather is the condition of the lower atmosphere at one time and in one place.

Weather conditions include air temperature, air pressure, precipitation, wind speed, wind direction, cloud and sun.

② key fact Climate is the average or expected pattern of weather for a place, based on weather records over a long time.

- A climate graph shows average monthly temperatures and rainfalls for a particular place.

- The data is collected over many years.

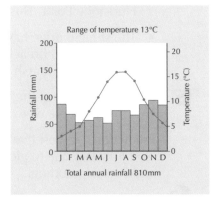

B World climate zones

① key fact The world is divided into major climatic zones. These are based on variations in precipitation and temperature between places.

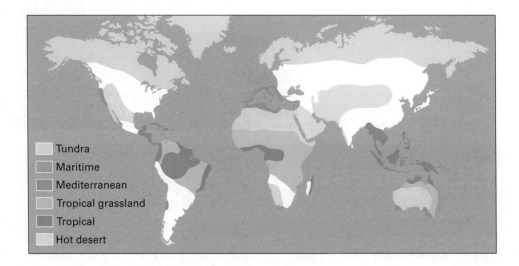

Tundra
Maritime
Mediterranean
Tropical grassland
Tropical
Hot desert

There are five main factors that affect climate:

Latitude

The angle of the sun and rotation of the Earth affect the temperature and climate of different parts of the world. The sun's rays hit the Earth overhead near the equator all year round, making these places hot. The sun's rays hit the poles at an oblique angle all year round, making these places cold. Whichever part of the Earth is tilted towards the sun experiences summer, while the other hemisphere gets winter.

study hint >>

Make sure you know which aspects of weather are in your course.

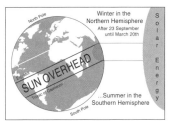
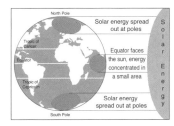
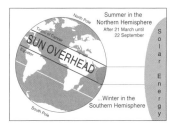

Continentality

The sea heats up more slowly and cools down more slowly than land. Places closer to the sea therefore have a smaller temperature range than those inland.

Altitude

Temperature decreases 0.6 °C every 100 m above sea level. In addition, places with hills experience greater rainfall due to relief.

Ocean currents

Currents spread warm water from the tropics to the poles and cold water from the poles to the tropics. This affects the temperature of air passing over the currents.

exam tip >>

Make sure you can plot temperature and rainfall as well as explain the patterns shown on a climate graph.

Prevailing wind

This is the most common wind in an area.
If the wind is tropical, it raises temperatures.
If the wind is polar, it lowers temperatures.

>> practice questions

1 **What is the difference between weather and climate?**

2 **Study the map and graphs of European climate.**

   a) **Why do July temperatures in Berlin and Rome differ?**

   b) **Why is the difference between summer and winter temperatures larger at Berlin than Shannon?**

   c) **Which place has the highest annual precipitation?**

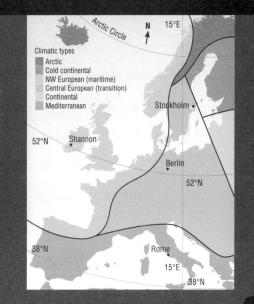

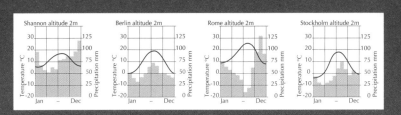

UK weather

 The UK's weather is heavily influenced by air masses.

 Other characteristics of the UK climate can be explained by its global position.

A Air masses

remember >>
Air masses create most UK weather patterns.

1 **key fact** Air masses are very large volumes of air with uniform temperature and humidity.

2 Where the air comes from and what it passes over influences the weather that the air mass brings. This is because air takes on some of the properties of the surfaces that it travels over.

3 **key fact** The UK has changeable weather because several different air masses affect the country.

Name of air mass: _Arctic Maritime_
Source region: _Arctic Circle_
Characteristics: _cold and wet_
Weather: _snow in winter_

Name of air mass: _Polar Maritime_
Source region: _Greenland Arctic Sea_
Characteristics: _wet and cold_
Weather: _cool and showers_

Name of air mass: _Polar continental_
Source region: _Central Europe + Siberia_
Characteristics: _cold in winter_
hot in summer
Weather: _some snow in winter, dry in summer_

Name of air mass: _Tropical Maritime_
Source region: _Mid-Atlantic_
Characteristics: _warm and moist_
Weather: _mild cloudy rain_

Name of air mass: _Tropical Continental_
Source region: _North Africa_
Characteristics: _hot and dry_
Weather: _hot in summer_

B Other factors influencing our weather and climate

As well as air masses, there are four other factors that affect Britain's climate:

Position

The UK is 50–58 °N of the equator. The sun's rays are spread obliquely over the UK, giving cool temperatures. The North gets less sunlight and is cooler than the South. The main wind direction is westerly.

Relief

Places at higher altitudes have lower temperatures and more rainfall.

Ocean currents

The Gulf Stream brings warm water (the North Atlantic Drift) from the Gulf of Mexico to the UK. The wind that blows over this water is warm, making winds from the west warmer. As this wind travels east across the UK it cools, making the east coast of the UK colder than the west coast.

Continentality

As the sea heats up and cools down slowly, places closer to the coast experience less extreme climates, with milder winters and cooler summers. Inland, the earth heats up and cools quickly, giving hotter summers but colder winters.

remember >>

Air masses create most of the UK's weather; climate is determined by the UK's global location.

exam tip >>

Make sure you can define these key words: maritime, continental, tropical, polar, Arctic.

>> practice questions

1 Which air masses bring rain?

2 Which air masses bring cold weather?

3 Which air masses are associated with the summer?

4 Why is the west coast of the UK warmer than the east coast?

Depressions and anticyclones

- Depressions are areas of low pressure that bring unsettled, cloudy, rainy weather.

- Anticyclones are areas of high pressure that bring calm, clear, dry weather.

A Depressions

1 key fact Depressions are areas of low pressure that develop to the west of the UK.

Depressions are associated with warm rising air. Depressions are created when a warm air mass and a cold air mass meet to form a front and are blown eastwards across the UK.

2 A depression forms when warm air rises up over cold air to form a warm front (shown as semicircles on a weather map). This results in less air at the surface, creating low pressure. The cold air behind the warm air forms a cold front (shown as triangles on a weather map). The cold front moves more quickly than the warm front and catches it up. The two fronts merge to form an occluded front (shown as alternate triangles and semicircles on a weather map).

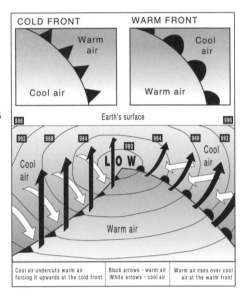

3 key fact The weather in a depression generally moves across the UK in a north-easterly direction and gives very changeable weather.

- As the warm front approaches, air pressure falls, it gets windy and starts to rain.

- As the warm sector passes over, air pressure and wind speed steady, it becomes warmer and it may stop raining.

- As the cold front approaches, air pressure rises but it becomes colder and windier and there is heavy rain.

- As the cold sector passes over, air pressure continues to rise, it remains cold and winds are squally with showers.

remember >>

If the two fronts meet and become occluded, the weather becomes very stormy.

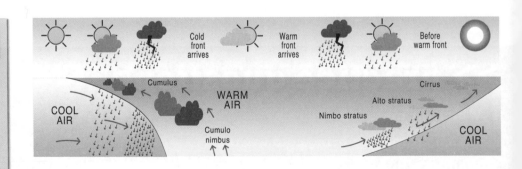

B Anticyclones

1 ![key fact] **An anticyclone is an area of high pressure.**

Anticyclones are associated with cool, sinking air. Anticyclones, or highs, bring settled weather that lasts for days or weeks and block out depressions.

2 An anticyclone forms when cold air sinks and warms, holding water vapour and preventing cloud formation. Winds are light and blow out from the centre of the high-pressure cell clockwise.

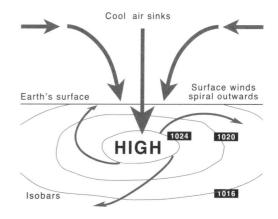

Cool air sinks

Earth's surface

Surface winds spiral outwards

HIGH 1024 1020

Isobars 1016

3 ![key fact] **Winter anticyclones bring cold, clear, sunny, settled weather.**

At night there is rapid heat loss as there are few clouds. This makes temperatures very cold. This can bring fog (which is dense cloud at ground level), mist (which is thin fog) and frost (which is frozen water droplets on the surface).

4 ![key fact] **Summer anticyclones bring hot, clear, sunny, settled weather.**

Temperatures often reach 25 °C. These high day temperatures can cause convection rainfall in late afternoon. Falling cool air can mix with smoke and pollution to produce smog over towns and cities. At night there is rapid heat loss as there are few clouds. This makes temperatures cold. This can bring morning dew, which is water vapour on the surface.

exam tip >>

Practising diagrams can help you revise a topic like weather.

>> practice questions

Study the satellite image and synoptic chart.

1 What type of weather is area A experiencing?

2 What type of weather is area B experiencing?

3 Pressure is high in area A and low in area B. From which direction is the wind blowing in the south of England?

4 Explain any similarities you can see between the cloud pattern shown on the satellite image and the pressure and fronts shown on the synoptic chart.

NB Isobars are the lines joining places of equal pressure (8 millibar intervals on this chart) – interpret them like contours.

Meteosat image of Europe

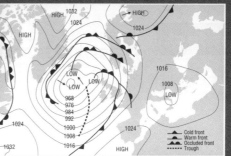

Weather map of Europe, based on satellite image above

Cold environments 1

- Cold environments are extreme.

- Polar and tundra landscapes are cold environments.

- Cold environments have limited flora and fauna; however, they are often home to valuable resources (e.g. oil).

- Many argue that cold environments are important wilderness areas that need careful management.

A The location of cold environments

>> **key fact** Polar and tundra environments are located in the far northern hemisphere and in the Antarctic region of the southern hemisphere.

- **Polar environments** are found at the Arctic and Greenland and on Antarctica. Polar areas increase dramatically in size in winter.

- The extent of polar areas is limited to the Arctic Circle 66.5 °N and the Antarctic Circle 66.5 °S.

- **Tundra environments** are found in northern Canada, Alaska, northern Russia, Iceland and some parts of Scandinavia.

B What are cold environments like and why?

① **key fact** Polar and tundra environments are covered in snow and ice for much of the year.

- In these environments, the climate is harsh, with long winters and short summers.

- There are snow storms and winds up to 90 km per hour for much of the year, and the average annual temperature range is –28 °C.

- As it is so cold, evaporation rates are very low and precipitation levels are also low – approximately 200 mm or less.

② Polar environments are covered by glaciers and ice sheets. These form through an accumulation of snow which then compresses and turns to ice.

- Ice moves due to gravity. As glaciers move, large cracks up to 60 m deep are formed. These are called crevasses.

- When an ice sheet grows out into the sea, it is called an ice shelf. If it breaks off, it becomes an iceberg.

③ **key fact** The ground in cold environments is called permafrost.

- The ground in polar environments is continuous permafrost as ground temperatures are below 0 °C all year round.

- In tundra environments there are patches of permafrost as the upper layer of the soil thaws in summer. The ground in this area is called discontinuous permafrost.

④ There are virtually no trees in cold environments.

In polar environments, algae, lichens and mosses are the most dominant plants. Vegetation in tundra environments also consists of lichens and mosses, but includes shrubs, grasses and forbs, which can grow 50–200 cm high. The amount of vegetation depends upon how much sun or snow cover is in the area.

⑤ **key fact** **Due to the harsh environment in cold areas, biodiversity is low. This means that there are few plants or animals.**

- In the Arctic, there are invertebrates including spiders, mites, mosquitoes and flies. Some of the larger animals that exist are polar bears, foxes, wolves, rabbits, shrews, reindeer and caribou.

- In the Antarctic, there are some invertebrates such as mites, fleas and ticks. Antarctica does not have any larger mammals but it does have penguins.

remember >>

Make sure you know the difference between the Arctic (Northern hemisphere) and the Antarctic (Southern hemisphere).

Penguins and the Antarctic environment

Cold environments 2

>> **key fact** Antarctica has no permanent residents, but indigenous people, the Inuit, have always lived and farmed in the Arctic.

Today, many cold environments are used for tourism, oil and mineral extraction and scientific research. These land uses can cause conflict between different interest groups.

Oil exploration in Alaska

- Prudhoe Bay, 70°N 148°W on the Arctic coast of Alaska in the USA, produces one million barrels of oil a day. The oilfield is located near the town of Deadhorse.
- The oil is sent for 1280 km along the Trans-Alaska pipeline to the port of Valdez, where it is shipped to the US.
- Oil exploitation has had negative impacts on the natural environment. Much wilderness was destroyed in the building of the oilfields and the pipeline. The overground oil pipes and industrial buildings are ugly and there have been leaks from corroding pipes. This is damaging natural habitats. The laying of huge pipes on the ground has disrupted the migratory patterns of caribou and other wildlife.
- Oil exploitation has had economic benefits. It has provided several thousand jobs in a region with few employment opportunities.

Tourism on Antarctica

- Antarctica received over 46 000 visitors in the 2007/8 season compared with 9000 in 1992/3. Over 50% of those visitors are from the US and the UK. This quantity of tourists creates huge potential environmental impacts.
- Although visitors spend only a short time on landings, it is a 'high impact' time as the numbers may damage the most beautiful and wildlife-rich areas of Antarctica. Most visitors arrive on small rafts from large cruise ships touring the area and land at the same sites along the Antarctic Peninsula.
- A Norwegian cruise ship ran aground on Deception Island in 2007. This raised concerns that these large ships present a dangerous environmental hazard if they are not ice-strengthened or staffed with experienced crew as they may leak oil if they crash. These ships also dump 'grey waste' and urine in open water or on ice.
- The introduction of alien species will also threaten the native ecosystem. On land, meadow grass and a flightless midge have been introduced on Signy Island and Mediterranean mussels have relocated in the Southern Ocean from the hulls of cruise ships.

Alaskan oil-drilling rig

Antarctic coastline

B How can cold environments be managed?

1 **key fact** Many people believe it is important to protect the world's cold environments. They are some of the last wilderness regions found on Earth and provide important sites of scientific research that can help explain the history of the Earth and climate change.

2 Forty-three countries have signed the Antarctic Treaty. This is a document which sets aside all claims to Antarctica and protects it as a place of science and peace. Some of the 'rules' set out in the Treaty include:

- Mining for minerals is banned until 2048.

- Fishing in the Southern Ocean is controlled.

- Rubbish must be removed and there are strict controls over what can be brought onto the continent.

- There has to be a unanimous decision by member nations on any new projects.

- Tourism is self-regulated by IAATO (International Association of Antarctic Tour Operators), which does not allow more than one cruise ship or 500 people to land at any one site at any one time and allows people no closer than 5 m to a penguin.

3 The Arctic is not protected by any treaties or protocols.

- However, an intergovernmental forum, the Arctic Council, has been set up to encourage cooperation between countries with interests in the Arctic.

- NGOs such as the World Wildlife Fund are active in publicising Arctic issues at a worldwide level.

exam tip >>
Learn as many facts and figures about your case studies as you can.

remember >>
Due to global warming, polar and tundra environments are changing rapidly.

>> practice questions

1 Where are cold environments found?

2 What is the climate like in a cold environment?

3 Briefly explain why there are few plants or animals found in a cold environment.

4 For either Prudhoe Bay or Antarctica, describe how the environment is being exploited.

5 Why is Antarctica managed more strictly than the Arctic?

Hot desert environments 1

- Hot desert and subtropical desert environments are found around the tropics.

- In hot desert environments rainfall is low, temperatures are high in the daytime, biodiversity is low and unique landforms are created.

- Hot desert environments have a number of traditional and modern land uses.

A The location of hot desert environments

1 **key fact** Hot desert or subtropical desert environments are found around the Tropics of Cancer (10–30 °N) and Capricorn (10–30 °S).

2 Hot deserts are found in six continents.

They include the Sonora desert in North America, the Kalahari, Namib and Sahara deserts in Africa, the Arabian and Thar deserts in Asia, the Atacama desert in South America and the Australian desert in Oceania. Generally, hot deserts are found in the west of a continent.

3 There are four types of hot desert: trade wind, rain shadow, coastal and monsoon.

B What are hot desert environments like and why?

1 **key fact** The hot desert environment has low rainfall.

This is because of high pressure. As the air sinks it gets drier, meaning few clouds and therefore little rain. Any rainfall is unreliable, so there could be years without rain.

2 **key fact** Daytime temperatures are high, at least 40 °C.

This heat leads to high rates of evaporation, making the atmosphere dry. Temperatures fall dramatically at night to below zero. This is because high pressure means clear skies which allow heat to escape into the atmosphere at night.

3 **key fact** Deserts are home to many unique and varied landscapes.

The main physical processes operating in the desert to create these landforms are:

- **weathering** (see pages 26–7), in particular insolation, weathering by block disintegration or exfoliation, freeze-thaw weathering and salt weathering

- **wind erosion** by deflation or abrasion

- **deposition** of eroded material.

4 These processes create the distinct landforms found in the desert.

Dunes in the Moroccan desert

5 Due to the harsh environment of the desert neither plants nor animals are abundant. Any plants or animals found there have had to devise ways to find and store water and cope with the heat. Some plants are ephemeral (e.g. the ocotillo). They lie dormant as seeds until rain comes and then they grow, flower and reproduce within a month. Other plants such as cacti are xerophytes. These obtain moisture from a wide, shallow root system and store water in their stems. They repel animals with spikes.

Ocotillo

Cactus

6 The main animals found in the desert are insects, spiders, reptiles and mammals such as the desert fox and the camel. Reptiles will avoid the heat by burrowing into the sand, and the fox is only active at night.

Hot desert environments 2

How do people use hot desert environments?

>> **key fact** Traditionally, people have used hot deserts for farming.

Nomads such as the Bedouin herd camels, goats, cattle and sheep and migrate from oasis to oasis to find vegetation for their animals to graze. Today, hot desert environments are also used for energy production, mineral extraction and tourism.

Oil exploration in Saudi Arabia

- Saudi Arabia is the world's largest producer of oil. This has brought wealth to the country and allowed health and education systems to develop to MEDC standard. The oilfields lie in the Arabian desert.

- Gharwar is the biggest oilfield on Earth and accounts for half of the entire oil production in Saudi Arabia and 6% of global production. It produces 5 million barrels a day. It is located 200 miles east of Riyadh.

- There are negative impacts, such as drilling hundreds of metres deep into the rock; construction of pipelines and buildings, which has disturbed wildlife and habitats; and the flares which burn off surplus oil and emit greenhouse gases can be seen from space.

Tourism in Uluru

- Uluru is located in the Northern Territory, central Australia. It lies 335 km south-west of the nearest large town, Alice Springs, 450 km by road. It lies within the Uluru–Kata Tjuta National Park. Uluru is sacred to the Pitjantjatjara and Yankunytjatjara, the Aboriginal people of the area, and is listed as a World Heritage Site.

- Uluru is visited by over 400 000 people a year, who come to experience the unique landscape and aboriginal culture.

- As well as economic benefits such as admission fees going to the Aboriginal community, there are negative impacts on both people and the environment. These include:

  - degradation of the natural environment through multiple visitor intrusion

  - pollution of land and waterways through inappropriate rubbish disposal and excessive noise

  - insensitivity toward indigenous culture

  - inefficient or inappropriate use of natural resources, including water.

Oil pipeline, Saudi Arabia

Uluru, Australia

B Managing the spread of deserts

① key fact Desertification is the degradation of dry land areas and the spread of desert conditions. It is caused by human activities and climate change.

Desertification threatens the Sahel, southern Europe, southern USA and parts of Asia. Land becomes degraded due to:

- the climate getting drier in these areas
- trees being used for firewood
- overgrazing leading to soil erosion
- overcultivation using up the soil's nutrients, making it infertile
- a growing population which needs food and fuel.

② The risk of desertification can be reduced if sustainable farming techniques are used. These are low-technology methods. They include:

- reducing stock density
- farming both animals and crops
- planting trees to protect the soil
- storing water by building earth dams, collecting water by using stone piles
- building low walls across fields to reduce run-off.

remember >>

A desert is an area that has an average rainfall of under 250 mm per year.

remember >>

Due to global warming, hot desert environments are changing rapidly.

>> practice questions

1 Match these deserts to their type

The Sahara is a …	monsoon desert
The Namib is a …	rain shadow desert
The Thar is a …	coastal desert
The Arabian is a …	trade wind desert

exam tip >>

Use precise terminology in your description of desert processes.

2 For either Uluru or Gharwar, describe how the environment is being exploited.

3 Describe how the farming techniques described above could help prevent the spread of deserts.

Climate change

- Some people believe that human activities in industrialised countries are changing the world's climate.

- The natural greenhouse effect is being altered.

- Global temperatures are rising, creating unpredictable weather systems and rising sea levels.

A The greenhouse effect

1 key fact The greenhouse effect is the way in which the atmosphere traps heat from the sun and warms the Earth's surface.

- Greenhouse gases such as carbon dioxide, nitrous oxide and methane absorb heat from the sun.

- This process keeps the surface of the Earth warm.

2 The greenhouse effect is a natural process and is vital for sustaining life on Earth.

Without the greenhouse effect, the Earth would be too cold for life.

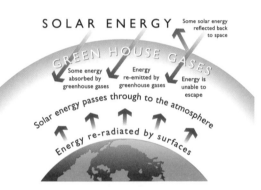

SOLAR ENERGY
Some solar energy reflected back to space

GREEN HOUSE GASES

Some energy absorbed by greenhouse gases

Energy re-emitted by greenhouse gases

Energy is unable to escape

Solar energy passes through to the atmosphere

Energy re-radiated by surfaces

B Global warming

1 Since the Industrial Revolution, humans have been emitting (releasing) more greenhouse gases to the atmosphere than occur naturally.

2 These gases trap additional heat. This enhances the greenhouse effect.

3 key fact The enhanced greenhouse effect could cause an overall rise in global temperatures, causing global warming.

remember >>

We need greenhouse gases to sustain life on Earth. However, for many years human activity has been producing extra greenhouse gases.

Methane is released into the atmosphere from farming and landfill sites.

Deforestation reduces the amount of trees available to convert carbon dioxide to oxygen.

Carbon dioxide is released into the atmosphere from factories, power stations and vehicles.

How does human activity generate greenhouse gases?

CFC gases or chlorofluorocarbons are released into the atmosphere from aerosols, old fridges and fast-food packaging.

Nitrous gases are released into the atmosphere from fertilisers.

C Evidence for and against human-led global warming

1 **key fact** Global warming is a controversial issue.

2 Some people argue that human-led global warming is not happening.

- Throughout history there have been natural cycles of warming and cooling on Earth.

- Evidence points to periods of very warm weather (e.g. the Medieval Warm Period) as well as periods of extremely cold weather (e.g. the Little Ice Age which occurred between the eleventh and fifteenth centuries).

- Some people believe that recent rises in global temperatures are simply part of a natural cycle of climate change.

- Natural events such as volcanic eruptions and variations in solar output can also alter the climate.

3 Despite these arguments, most scientists agree that human activity has caused the warming that we are now experiencing.

Many scientists argue that the scale and speed at which temperatures are rising is evidence of human-led global warming. They also believe that the impacts of rising temperatures will be more severe than in the past.

4 **key fact** Reports suggest that global temperatures have increased by 0.6 °C in the past 100 years.

- Some people believe that a rise in average temperatures of 2 °C would be the tipping point for triggering dangerous climate change. Others argue that it is as low as 1 °C.

- Organisations such as the United Nations Intergovernmental Panel on Climate Change (IPCC) monitor changes in land and sea temperatures. They collect historical temperature records using ice cores and make predictions for future climate change.

- Recent evidence for human-led climate change includes retreating glaciers and shrinking ice-cover in the Arctic.

> **study hint >>**
> Make sure you can explain the greenhouse effect and show how it contributes to global warming.

>> practice questions

1 **What is the greenhouse effect?**

2 **Using examples, explain how human activity can increase greenhouse gas emissions.**

3 **Why are people uncertain about the causes of global warming?**

Managing the impacts of climate change

- Global warming could have serious impacts on people and places.

- Global temperatures appear to be rising, creating unpredictable weather systems and rising sea levels.

- People can take steps to reduce the impacts of global warming.

A The impacts of global warming

1 **key fact** Those who believe that global warming is taking place are very concerned about the impacts that it may have, now and in the future.

2 The impacts of global warming may affect people, the environment and the economy.

3 Many scientists believe that evidence of global warming can already be seen:

- Sea levels appear to be rising due to polar ice caps melting.

- Sea levels rose 25 cm in the past 100 years and are set to rise by a further 50 cm by 2100.

- Rising sea levels could cause low-lying parts of the world like the Ganges Delta in Bangladesh and southern England to flood permanently.

- The thickness of glaciers in the Alps appears to be diminishing fast. Many glaciers appear to be retreating.

- In 2002, 3200 sq km of ice shelf broke away from the Antarctic Peninsula.

- Coral reefs such as the Great Barrier Reef are experiencing record levels of bleaching.

- Extreme weather events like hurricanes appear to be getting more frequent.

4 In the future, global warming could change the world's climate zones.

- Dry areas like the Sahara could spread further north to Europe.

- Cold areas like Alaska could warm up and sustain agriculture.

5 Weather patterns may change. Britain could become much wetter in winter and much warmer in summer.

6 Flooding is a major challenge posed by global warming. As well as rising sea levels causing flooding in low-lying areas, extreme weather may also greatly increase the risk of flooding in many parts of the world including the UK.

B Slowing down the impacts of global warming

1 This could be achieved by reducing the number of greenhouse gases in the atmosphere, particularly carbon dioxide. This could be done by:

- Increasing afforestation (planting trees) and reducing deforestation.

- Using more sustainable sources of energy production that do not rely upon burning fossil fuels (e.g. wind power).

- Reducing our use of energy and other resources. Waste needs to be managed and wherever resources can be reused, this creates less demand for manufacturing from new raw materials.

- Research and investment can take place to help develop new more fuel-efficient technology.

key fact **Global warming needs to be tackled at local, national and global levels.**

- Locally, individuals can try to reduce their carbon footprint (the amount of carbon dioxide emissions they are responsible for). This can be done by offsetting flights, using sustainable forms of transport and conserving energy at home.

- Internationally, countries can co-operate with each other by signing agreements to reduce greenhouse gas emissions.

The Kyoto Agreement, signed in 1997, is an example of an international agreement.

- Despite signing the Kyoto Agreement, the USA has since backed down on its commitment to reduce emissions, claiming that to do so would lower their standard of living.

- The Kyoto Agreement was followed up by the Washington Declaration in 2007.

- The Washington Declaration suggested a system that caps (limits) a country's carbon dioxide emissions. Each country is given a carbon emissions allowance (or carbon credits); they are able to trade these credits with other countries.

- Often carbon trading involves high-polluting countries buying a share of the emissions allowance from a less-polluting country. Some LEDCs feel that this is not fair.

- Some LEDCs argue that capping carbon dioxide emissions could slow down their rate of development and they do not want to pay their own economic price for a global problem that they feel MEDCs created.

> **remember >>**
>
> The Arctic and Antarctica are two different places (the Arctic is in the northern hemisphere, Antarctica is in the southern hemisphere). Also, look carefully at their spelling.

> **remember >>**
>
> Global warming may directly affect Britain.

>> practice questions

1 **Describe three possible impacts of global warming.**

2 **Explain how people can try to slow down the impacts of global warming.**

3 **Managing global warming is complicated and complex. Explain why.**

Ecosystems

- An ecosystem is an ecological system.

- All the parts of an ecosystem interact with each other and are interdependent.

- Ecosystems have inputs, processes and outputs.

- There are two important processes within an ecosystem: energy flows and nutrient cycles.

A What is an ecosystem?

① key fact An ecosystem is an ecological system.

② An ecosystem is a system of plants and animals that live together in a particular environment. The animals and plants interact with each other and their surrounding environment.

③ The size of an ecosystem can vary from very large to very small. A garden pond is an ecosystem and so is a tropical rainforest.

④ The world's largest ecosystems are called biomes.

remember >>

You have probably studied ecosystems in science. Your science work may give some more case studies of different ecosystems.

- Tropical rainforest
- Desert/Semi-desert
- Tundra
- Coniferous forest
- Deciduous forest
- Temperate grasslands
- Mediterranean/scrubland
- Mountainous
- Polar

B How do ecosystems work?

① key fact The living parts of an ecosystem are called biotic. The non-living parts of an ecosystem are called abiotic.

② The living and non-living parts of an ecosystem interact with each other. They are interdependent, which means that they depend on each other to make the system work.

③ key fact If one part of the ecosystem is altered, the whole system will be affected.

The abiotic (non-living) part of the ecosystem provides the environment that helps plants and animals of the ecosystem to survive.

④ Like many other geographical systems, an ecosystem has inputs, processes and outputs (see the river system, page 31).

The greater the inputs into the ecosystem, the greater the biodiversity of plants and animals supported by the ecosystem. For example, a desert has limited inputs of rain and soil nutrients and so the range of vegetation and wildlife found in a desert is small.

⑤ There are two important processes within an ecosystem: nutrient cycles and energy flows.

- Sometimes the flows within an ecosystem are shown using arrows. The arrows show the direction of the flow and how great the flow is. The wider or larger the arrow, the greater the flow of nutrients of energy.

Nutrient cycles

- Nutrients are found naturally in the rocks, water and the atmosphere.

- Nutrients are important minerals such as nitrogen, magnesium, calcium, phosphorous and potassium. These nutrients are essential to all living things.

- The nutrient cycle moves these minerals through the ecosystem.

- Decomposers, such as small bacteria and fungi, break up dead leaves and organisms and return the nutrients to the soil, to be taken up by plants and trees.

- Nutrients may be lost from the ecosystem. This may happen if the nutrients are washed away by surface run-off or through leaching. Leaching occurs when the nutrients are washed down to the lower layers of the soil, where they can't be reached by plants or trees.

remember >>

Within an ecosystem there are other smaller systems at work, for example the nutrient cycle.

Energy flows

- Energy flows through an ecosystem through the food chain.

- Many ecosystems provide valuable resources for humans. Sometimes these resources are not used sustainably. This can harm the ecosystem.

All energy comes from the sun. Plants are **producers**, making plant food (glucose) through photosynthesis.	Herbivores eat plants. These are **primary consumers**.	Herbivores are eaten by carnivores. These are **secondary consumers**.	Energy is lost when plants and animals breathe. More energy is lost higher up the chain.

>> practice questions

1 Use the map opposite to name three types of ecosystem.

2 Briefly explain why there are few plants or animals found in a desert ecosystem.

3 With reference to a named ecosystem, explain how energy flows through the system.

exam tip >>

Make sure you can draw a food chain for an ecosystem that you have studied

The rainforest ecosystem 1

- Rainforest ecosystems are found close to or along the equator.

- Rainforests are found in areas of tropical climate. This provides the system with high inputs of rain and sun.

- Rainforest ecosystems can support a rich diversity of plant and animal species.

A The location of tropical rainforests

>> **key fact** Tropical rainforests are found in a belt 5° north or south of the equator.

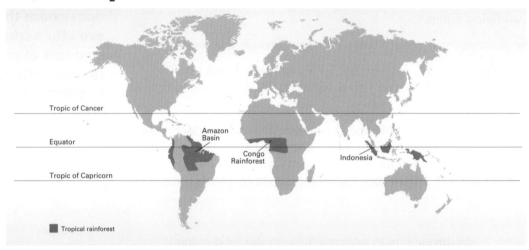

Tropic of Cancer

Equator

Amazon Basin

Congo Rainforest

Indonesia

Tropic of Capricorn

■ Tropical rainforest

B How does the rainforest ecosystem work?

1 The average daily temperature in the rainforest is between 25–30°C, while the average yearly rainfall is between 1500mm and 3000mm.

2 This means that the rainforest ecosystem has very high inputs of rain and sun. The atmosphere is very moist and humid.

3 **key fact** These conditions are excellent for plant growth, which means that rainforests have a high diversity of plants, insects, birds and animals.

4 Nutrient cycling in the rainforest is very rapid, because the humid conditions help dead matter to decompose quickly. There is also a vast network of bacteria and fungi that helps break down dead material and return nutrients to the soil. These nutrients help to support the plant and animal species in the forest.

5 The structure of the rainforest is very important in helping the ecosystem to function. Rainforests have distinct layers of vegetation.

remember >>

If you are describing the location of the world's rainforests, name specific places, such as the Amazon rainforest (Brazil).

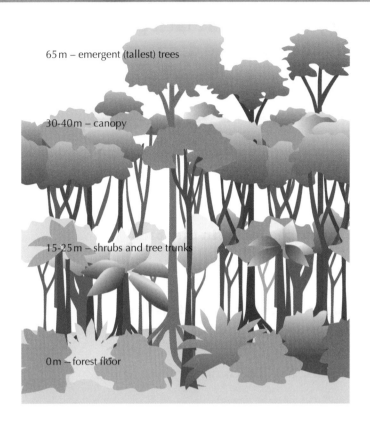

65 m – emergent (tallest) trees

30-40 m – canopy

15-25 m – shrubs and tree trunks

0 m – forest floor

The emergents: These are the tallest trees that have emerged out of the canopy layer. These trees can grow up to 65 metres tall.

The canopy: This layer forms the 'roof' of the forest. The trees are up to 40 metres tall and have grown high upwards in search of light. Small climbing plants, such as lianas, are often wrapped around the trunks of these trees.

The lower canopy: Here are the youngest trees and saplings. It is still quite dark here and the trees are fighting for the light.

The forest floor: Here there is less vegetation due to the dark, damp conditions. This layer has a thick layer of decomposing leaves and is home to the large buttress roots of the largest trees.

C Why are rainforests being destroyed?

1 **key fact** The rainforest ecosystems are under threat from destruction by humans. Many countries and businesses want to take advantage of and exploit the resources of the forest.

2 The Amazon rainforest is the world's largest rainforest and areas of it are being destroyed as people make use of its resources.

remember >>

Rainforest ecosystems rely on high inputs. These inputs help create a very rich and diverse ecosystem.

Logging: Expensive wood, such as mahogany, is cut down by logging companies and exported across the world.

Roads and buildings: Land in the forest needs to be cleared to make space for industrial buildings, accommodation for the workers and for building roads to get goods in and out of the region.

Reasons for the destruction of the Amazon rainforest

Cattle ranching: Large areas of the forest have been cleared for raising cattle, which can then be sold for their meat.

Mining: In the Amazon there are huge reserves of minerals such as gold, iron ore and copper. These are used in industries throughout the world. To get at these minerals, vast stretches of the forest must be destroyed and mines excavated.

The rainforest ecosystem 2

The diversity of the rainforest ecosystem means that it provides humans with many resources. This has led to the destruction of many rainforest areas.

A What are the impacts of human activity in rainforest areas?

1 **key fact** In order to exploit the resources found in the forest, trees are often removed. This is called deforestation.

2 **key fact** Cutting down trees in the rainforest can destroy the ecosystem. If one part of the system is removed, it can no longer work or function properly.

Removing trees in order to develop areas of rainforest has impacts on the environment, people and the economy.

3 The nutrient cycle moves these minerals through the ecosystem:

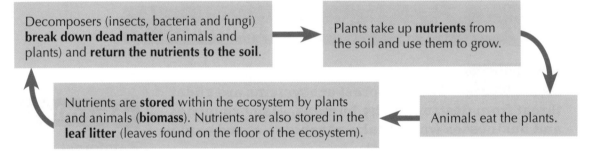

If trees are removed, the cycle is broken. The soil becomes infertile and nutrients stored in the soil are washed away by the rain. This is called leaching. Removal of trees leaves the soil exposed, causing erosion by wind or rain.

4 Removing trees from a tropical rainforest affects the amount and type of plant and animal species in the ecosystem. Deforestation destroys animal habitats and reduces the flow of energy within the system. Over time, plant and animal species may reduce in number and eventually become extinct. Some species of rainforest vegetation provide humans with many common household medicines. Some experts believe that certain rainforest plants could provide cures for disease.

5 Many scientists believe that deforestation of rainforests could lead to changes in the world's climate. Trees absorb carbon dioxide and give out oxygen. Cutting down trees alters the balance of gases in the atmosphere. Increased greenhouse gases such as carbon dioxide adds to the problem of global warming.

6 Rainforest developments can affect local people. People may be forced to leave the area and set up home elsewhere. This can put pressure on settlements found close to the forest. Local communities may be broken up and cultural traditions lost. However, there may be some positive impacts for local people. They may gain employment from the development of the rainforest. This could raise their income.

remember >>

Not all of the world's rainforests are being destroyed. In places where the forests are being destroyed, people cannot agree on how fast this is happening.

7 Developing rainforest areas and exploiting their resources can help to boost local and national economies. Jobs are created and income can be generated from exporting rainforest products, e.g. hardwood. However, if rainforest development is not sustainable, people may not benefit from the forest in the long term.

B How can the rainforests be managed?

1 **key fact** Scientists cannot agree on how fast the world's rainforests are being destroyed.

- Some people predict that if we continue to remove trees from the world's rainforest ecosystems, the forests will have disappeared within the next hundred years. However, some experts disagree with this view and argue that there are many large areas of undisturbed rainforest across the world.

- Although people can't agree on how fast the world's rainforests are being destroyed, more and more governments and international organisations have begun to realise their importance.

2 Rainforests supply the world with a valuable supply of oxygen and contain important plant and animal species. Therefore, measures have been taken to protect the world's rainforest ecosystems:

- Sustainable logging is taking place in many areas. Once a tree is cut down, another is planted.

- Areas of rainforest have been designated as protected areas, where no development can take place. Ecotourism may be used to generate income in protected areas. The money from ecotourism is often invested in protecting the area further.

- People have been educated about the importance of the rainforest and consumers in MEDCs are given information about where the wood they buy has come from.

- In parts of the Amazon, mining companies are required to replant trees once they have finished mining the area.

exam tip **>>**

If you are asked to write about a rainforest ecosystem, make sure you name the rainforest you are writing about.

Australian rainforest, Blue Mountains

>> practice questions

1 Use the map on page 70 to describe the distribution of the world's rainforests.

2 Give two reasons for the rich diversity of wildlife in the rainforest ecosystem.

3 For a named ecosystem that you have studied, explain why humans have changed the ecosystem and describe what impact this has had on the environment.

Population change

- The world's population is rising rapidly. It reached six billion in 1999.

- Population growth is caused by differences between births and deaths.

- Population growth is highest in LEDCs.

A Population growth

1 **key fact** The world's population is growing rapidly.

Billions — Start of rapid growth period — 1500 1600 1700 1800 1900 2000

2 For thousands of years, the world's population grew at a steady rate.

- In 1820, the world's population reached one billion.

- In 1999, less than two hundred years later, the world's population totalled six billion.

- Since the 1960s, the world's population has been growing at a rate of one billion every 15 years or so.

- This rapid rise in the world's population has been called a 'population explosion'.

3 There are three causes of population change:

Births	measured using the birth rate (number of live births per 1000 of the population)
Deaths	measured using the death rate (number of deaths per 1000 of the population)
Migration	the movement of people in and out of a country

4 The difference between the birth rate and the death rate of a country is called the rate of natural population increase.

- If the birth rate is higher than the death rate, the total population will increase.

- If the death rate is higher than the birth rate, the total population will decrease.

5 **key fact** Population growth rates are highest in LEDCs where birth rates are high, but death rates are falling across the world. Death rates are falling due to global improvements in health and medicine.

remember >>

The world's population is growing rapidly because birth rates are still very high in LEDCs, while death rates are falling across the world.

B The demographic transition model

1 The demographic transition model opposite shows population change over time. It is divided into five stages.

2 As a country passes through the stages of the model, the total population increases. Most MEDCs are in stage four or five of the model; most LEDCs are currently at stage two or three.

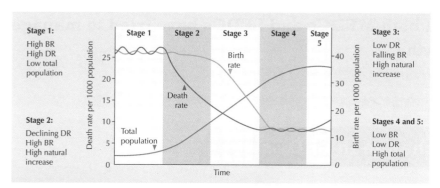

Stage 1:
High BR
High DR
Low total population

Stage 2:
Declining DR
High BR
High natural increase

Stage 3:
Low DR
Falling BR
High natural increase

Stages 4 and 5:
Low BR
Low DR
High total population

C Population structure

1 Population structure refers to the way in which the population of an area is divided up between males and females of different age groups.

2 **key fact** **Population pyramids are used to show population structure.**

- Population pyramids can be drawn for a whole country or individual settlements (towns or villages).

- The shape of a population pyramid gives us information about birth rates, death rates and life expectancy in a country or settlement. Life expectancy is how long, on average, a person can expect to live.

- A population pyramid also tells us about the number of dependants living in an area. Young dependants (under 15) and elderly dependants (over 65) depend on the economically active (those of working age).

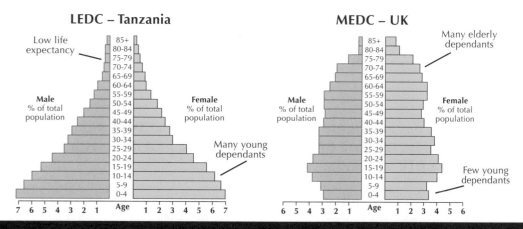

>> practice questions

1 **What is meant by natural population increase?**

2 **Describe the main changes that take place as a country moves through the demographic transition model.**

3 **How does the number of dependants differ between the population of UK and Tanzania?**

Managing population change

- The population of many LEDCs is growing rapidly.
- The population of some MEDCs is declining.
- Governments in both MEDCs and LEDCs have tried to manage population growth.

A Population change in LEDCs

1 key fact The population of most LEDCs is rising rapidly.

2 Most LEDCs are now at stage two or three in the demographic transition model (see page 77). They have high birth rates and falling death rates. This means that LEDCs have a high rate of natural increase.

3 Death rates are falling due to modern improvements in health care and medicine.

4 There are several reasons for high birth rates in LEDCs:

- It may not be culturally or religiously acceptable to use contraception.

- Lack of contraception.

- High rates of infant deaths (infant mortality) results in women having more children to ensure that some survive through to adulthood.

- Limited education about family planning.

- It may be traditional to have large families.

- Children may be needed to earn money or farm the land.

exam tip >>

In your exam, make sure you read questions carefully and check if you are being asked to write about an LEDC or MEDC.

5 The high rate of population growth in LEDCs means there are many young dependants. This creates problems for LEDCs. As they grow older, these dependants will need housing, healthcare and employment.

6 key fact The governments and aid charities in LEDCs want to reduce birth rates, slow down the rate of population growth and deal with the growing impact of HIV and Aids.

Case study – Managing population change in Tanzania

Tanzania is located in East Africa. It has a total population of around 40 million.

The birth rate is 38. This is higher than the death rate of 15 and so it has a rate of natural increase of 2.3% each year. This rate would be even higher if the infant mortality rate of 75 were lower.

If the population of Tanzania continues to grow at the current rate of natural increase, it will reach at least 82 million by the year 2050, an increase of 105%.

Derada is a village in Tanzania where attempts have been made to manage population growth.

- Many of the women in Derada have had large families. Many young children in the village die before their fifth birthday and the use of contraception is not traditionally acceptable.

- The local authorities and charities working in the area have tried to reduce the birth rate in Derada. A local health clinic has been built where children are vaccinated against childhood diseases and women are offered advice about contraception and family planning.

- These changes have meant that rates of infant mortality (infant deaths) have fallen and women are having smaller families. Women are also able to plan when they have children and complete their education.

B Population change in MEDCs

1. The population growth rate of most MEDCs is stable. MEDCs tend to have low birth rates and low death rates.

2. The population of some MEDCs is actually declining. For example, in Italy the birth rate is lower than the death rate and it has a natural decrease of 7000 people each year.

3. **key fact** One of the biggest issues facing MEDCs is the problem of an ageing population.

   As modern healthcare becomes more advanced and the standard of living in MEDCs rises, people are living longer. This means that many MEDCs will have a high number of elderly dependants who need to be provided with healthcare, public transport services and suitable housing.

4. In some MEDCs the government is trying to increase the population growth rate to help pay for the ageing population. They have done this by providing incentives for young people to consider starting a family, e.g. paid maternity leave and tax incentives.

Case study – Managing population change in Japan

Japan is located off the coast of China in the Pacific Ocean. It has a population of 128 million.

The birth rate is 9. This is equal to the death rate so it currently has a zero rate of natural increase each year.

It is predicted that the population of Japan will decrease by 25% to 95 million by the year 2050. This is because women in Japan give birth to 1.3 children on average, which is below the number needed to replace the population.

This presents challenges to the Japanese government as there will be fewer people of working age to support those aged over 65 (currently 22% of the population). By 2025 there will be only two people of working age for every elderly dependant. Japan is meeting these challenges by:

- Encouraging women to have more babies. The 'new angel' policy supports women who return to work and pays for infertility treatment. This is raising birth rates.

- Reforming the pension scheme in 2004. People have to pay higher premiums and from 2030 will have to be at least 65 before they can retire.

- Legislating to allow companies to employ workers beyond the legal retirement age. Today 30% of people aged over 60 work.

- Introducing a compulsory insurance scheme to pay for long-term residential care for the elderly.

>> practice questions

1 Why are many LEDCs experiencing rapid population growth?

2 With reference to a named example, explain how population growth can be controlled.

3 What is an ageing population?

4 How is Japan dealing with the issues of an ageing society?

Migration

- Migration is the movement from one place to go to live in another.

- Migration can be explained by 'push' and 'pull' factors.

- Some people are forced to leave their home due to war or natural disasters. These people are called refugees.

A Types of migration

1 There are several different types of migration:

Internal migration is when people move within a region or country.

International migration is when people move from one country to another.

Voluntary migration is when people choose to move, perhaps for a better lifestyle or job.

Forced migration is when people are forced to move home, perhaps due to a natural hazard or war.

2 People who migrate are called migrants.

- **Emigration** is when someone leaves a country.
- **Immigration** is when someone moves into a country.
- **Net immigration** is the number of immigrants minus the number of emigrants.
- **Migration** can be permanent or temporary.

3 Many countries now have laws and policies to control the number of people immigrating into the country. Australia uses a points-based system. Emigrants have to score a certain number of points to gain entry to Australia as a migrant. Points are awarded for a range of criteria, such as good health, age, possessing skills that are needed (e.g. nursing). Other countries including the UK are trying to introduce similar schemes.

B Push and pull factors

1 **key fact** Migration is usually caused by a combination of push and pull factors.

- Push factors are the reasons why someone wants or needs to leave an area.
- Pull factors are the reasons that attract someone to a new area.

Push Factors: unemployment, crop failure, lack of services and amenities, drought, flooding, war, poverty

Pull Factors: employment opportunities, better housing, better services and amenities, better education and healthcare. Pull factors may be based on migrants' perceptions.

2 For international migrants, the country that a migrant leaves behind is known as the source country, and where they move to is known as the host or receiving country.

3 When a large number of people leave an area, it is called depopulation.

C International migration within the European Union

1 The European Union is an economic and political union. In 2009 it had 27 member states or nations.

For residents of the EU, movement between member states is relatively easy.

2 Throughout the 1990s and in the early 2000s, several Eastern European countries joined the EU.

- After these countries had joined the EU, some of their residents migrated to other parts of Europe in search of work.

- Many of these economic migrants settled in Western Europe in countries such as the UK.

3 It is very hard to keep an accurate record of the number of migrants arriving in a country. Some may come illegally; these are not registered with the authorities.

- Reports suggest that in 2004, after 10 new member states joined the EU, 50,000 migrants came to the UK. Some people estimate it was much higher, at 130,000.

- A large number of EU migrants migrating to the UK have come from Poland; however, many have now returned home.

4 Migration has positive and negative impacts on both the source and host countries. For example, migrants fill important gaps in the labour market in the host country and may work for lower wages than local people. They may also send money (called remittances) home to relatives living in the source country. However, the arrival of migrants may cause tension within communities. The economy of the source country may also suffer as young, skilled workers leave the country to live elsewhere.

5 It is hard to manage migration within the EU, due to 'open borders' policies between member states.

D Refugees

1 **key fact** **Refugees are people who have been forced to leave their home.**

2 Refugees may be forced to leave due to war, political or religious conflict or natural hazards such as floods.

3 Most refugees move to a nearby region or country. For example, due to conflict in Sudan, many thousands of people have fled to neighbouring Chad. Some refugees move further away to countries where they feel they will be offered political tolerance and the chance of a better quality of life. For example, during the Kosovan conflict, many refugees applied for asylum in the UK and other European countries.

4 In 2005, there were estimated to be 8.4 million refugees in the world.

>> practice questions

1 **What is meant by net migration?**

2 **Using examples, explain what is meant by push factors.**

3 **For a named example you have studied, explain the impacts of international migration on both the source and host country.**

Urban settlement

- An urban settlement is a built-up area, usually a town or city.
- The world is becoming increasingly urban.
- Many LEDCs are urbanising rapidly.

A Global patterns of urbanisation

① key fact Urbanisation means an increase in the proportion of people living in urban areas (towns or cities) compared with rural areas.

- You can measure levels of urbanisation by calculating the percentage of the total population living in urban areas.

- In 1900, only about 10% of the world's population lived in urban areas. The UN estimates that today, 50% of the world's population live in urban areas. The world is now urbanised.

② As a country industrialises it tends to become more urbanised. Most MEDCs industrialised many years ago and so they already have large urban populations. Many LEDCs are in the early stages of industrialisation; they tend to have a growing urban population.

study hint >>

Make sure you understand how rates of urbanisation differ between MEDCs and LEDCs.

- MEDCs tend to have high levels of urbanisation, e.g. 90% of people in the UK live in urban areas.

- LEDCs tend to have low levels of urbanisation, e.g. approximately 30% of people in India live in urban areas.

- However, most LEDCs are urbanising very rapidly. For example, in India the rate of urban growth is estimated to be 2.36% compared with 0.51% in the UK.

B Urban land use

① There are four main land uses common to most cities:

Commercial, business and administrative land uses (e.g. shops, offices and banks). 	Industrial land uses (e.g. factories and small production centres).
Residential land use (e.g. housing).	Open land (e.g. parkland and sports grounds). 

Each of these different land uses tend to be found in particular area or zone.

② key fact The way in which these land uses are arranged within a town or city tends to differ between MEDCs and LEDCs.

C Land-use patterns in MEDC cities

remember >>

All cities are different and land use models can only give us a general idea about a particular city.

1 To help us understand land use within cities, geographers have drawn models of a 'typical' urban settlement. These models are simplified versions of what cities are really like and they make many generalisations.

2 One of the most famous urban land use models is the Burgess model.

- The Burgess model is based on a pattern of concentric rings. Each ring represents a land use zone.

- Land values fall as you move from the centre of the city – the central business district or CBD. This theory of declining land values with distance from the CBD is called distance decay.

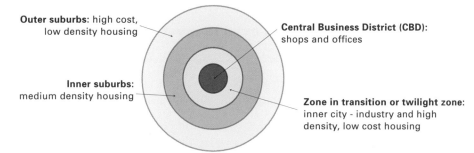

Outer suburbs: high cost, low density housing

Central Business District (CBD): shops and offices

Inner suburbs: medium density housing

Zone in transition or twilight zone: inner city - industry and high density, low cost housing

D Land-use patterns in LEDC cities

1 LEDC cities tend to have a similar land use zones to MEDCs. However, they are arranged differently.

In LEDCs, areas of high- and middle-class housing tend to be found just outside the CBD. The poorer-quality housing is found on the edge of the city (the opposite of MEDC cities).

2 **key fact** The areas of poorer-quality housing found on the edge of the city are called squatter settlements or shanty towns.

3 The model below shows the general pattern of land use in a typical LEDC city.

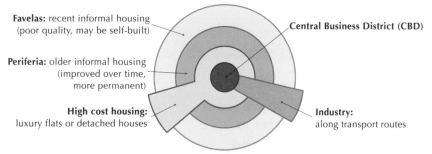

Favelas: recent informal housing (poor quality, may be self-built)

Central Business District (CBD)

Periferia: older informal housing (improved over time, more permanent)

High cost housing: luxury flats or detached houses

Industry: along transport routes

>> practice questions

1 **How do rates of urbanisation vary between LEDCs and MEDCs?**

2 **Describe the typical land-use pattern in an MEDC city.**

3 **Describe the typical land-use pattern in an LEDC city.**

Challenges facing MEDC cities

- Many areas of MEDC cities have been regenerated and redeveloped in recent decades.

- Many MEDC cities face challenges of traffic congestion and pollution.

- In some areas 'eco-cities' are being built in order to address some of the social and environmental challenges we face.

A Inequalities within cities

1 **key fact** Socio-economic areas exist in most urban areas.

2 The inequalities found in urban areas include:

- **Access to housing** – housing standards vary within towns and cities. Some people do not have access to good-quality, safe housing. In some areas there is a lack of affordable housing.

- **Access to services and amenities** – services, e.g. medical centres, are not always distributed evenly across urban areas. The quality of services can also vary greatly. For example, some people do not have access to a reliable bus service.

- **Quality of life** – standards of living vary in towns and cities. In some areas there are concentrations of wealth, in others there can be high levels of deprivation.

- **Environmental quality** – some urban areas are very attractive, with open spaces, greenery and low levels of litter, crime and vandalism. In areas of deprivation, the opposite is often the case.

3 Inequalities may exist between particular individuals or groups living in urban areas. The elderly, disabled, particular ethnic groups or those living on a low income may be more disadvantaged than others.

4 Statistics such as census data can be used to investigate and map urban inequalities.

5 Local and national governments may work with local businesses and charities to reduce inequalities in urban areas. Initiatives have been introduced to improve access to services and educational attainment in inner city areas, e.g. City Challenge in the UK and other parts of Europe.

B Urban redevelopment and regeneration

1 **key fact** Over the past 30 years local and national governments and private companies have tried to redevelop and regenerate parts of MEDC towns and cities.

In the UK, much of this redevelopment and regeneration has taken place in inner-city areas.

2 Inner-city areas developed during the industrial revolution when MEDC cities began to grow outwards. Factories and industry developed close to the CBD. Small Victorian terraced homes were built nearby to house the factory workers.

study hint >>

You may have studied a particular redevelopment and regeneration project. You need to be able to say why it was needed, what it involved and how successful it was.

- During the 19th century large numbers of people moved from the countryside to the city looking for work (rural–urban migration). Most migrants found work in the factories. The inner city became densely populated and living conditions were poor.

- Since the Second World War, the inner city has seen many changes. Traditional manufacturing industry has declined and most of the factories have closed. This has left the inner city with many problems.

- During the 1950s and 60s, the UK government cleared many inner-city areas, by demolishing old houses and factories. This was called slum clearance. Many people were rehoused in new high-rise flats or moved to housing estates on the edge of town.

- During the 1980s and 90s many inner-city areas were redeveloped. Redevelopment involves improving the physical environment of an area. In the inner-city new offices, houses and flats were built. Redevelopment tends to attract new business and investment into an area, which in turn helps create employment opportunities and raise people's quality of life. This is known as regeneration.

3 Redeveloping land that was once used for housing or industry is called brownfield development. Many interest groups and councils are in favour of such development because it helps to protect greenfield sites and prevents urban sprawl. However, brownfield sites can be costly to develop and contaminated land can be an issue.

4 Schemes to improve decaying urban areas can have both costs and benefits. It is important to look at these when evaluating the success of a particular scheme.

C Transport problems in cities

1 **key fact** **Many MEDC towns and cities were developed before the widespread use of cars and buses. This means that they were not designed for heavy use of cars and other vehicles.**

Today, people use many different modes of transport to move around cities, e.g. bus, car, train, tram, bicycle, foot and motorbike.

2 Congestion is now a major problem in many cities, particularly in the CBD. There are several causes of this traffic congestion:

- As cities have grown outwards and urban sprawl has taken place, large roads and motorways have been built on the edge of many cities. These link up with other smaller roads that bring cars into the city centre. Many of the roads in the inner parts of the city tend to be narrow and in need of regular maintenance.

- Many people now live on the edge of cities and commute (travel) to the city each day for work.

- Most cities are now major route centres. This means that several different routes (road and rail) all converge (meet) in the city. This has created problems of congestion and pollution.

- During recent years the government and local councils have tried to reduce the problems of traffic congestion in cities. Different traffic management schemes have been introduced in cities and towns, e.g. park and ride schemes. Some schemes have been more successful than others.

>> practice questions

1 Outline two inequalities that may be experienced by those who live in cities.

2 Explain why inner-city areas in MEDCs are often areas of decline.

3 Describe and explain how the environment and economy of inner-city areas can be improved.

Challenges facing LEDC cities

- Rapid urbanisation is taking place in many LEDCs.

- Many people in LEDC cities live in vast squatter settlements found on the edge of the city.

- The conditions in squatter settlements are poor but in many cities improvements are being made to these areas.

A The causes of rapid urban growth in LEDCs

1 There are two main causes of rapid urbanisation in LEDCs:

- Rural-to-urban migration (the movement of people from the countryside to cities).

- High rates of natural increase in urban areas. This is due to high birth rates (migrants tend to be of child-bearing age) and falling death rates (due to improved access to healthcare facilities) and leads to a high natural increase in the population.

2 Push and pull factors can be used to help explain why people in LEDCs are migrating from the countryside to urban areas.

Push factors (encouraging people to leave rural areas)	**Pull factors** (attracting people to urban areas)
Unemployment	Greater number and variety of employment opportunities
Low wages	Higher wages
Unprofitable farming	Chances to improve their standard of living
Few employment opportunities	Better schools and hospitals
The need to support a growing population (population pressure)	Better housing and basic services (water, electricity, sewerage)
Lack of social amenities and leisure	Opportunities for a better social and cultural life
	Better transport and communications

B Squatter settlements

1 Rural–urban migrants in LEDCs tend to settle on the edge of the city in squatter settlements.

Squatter settlements are usually illegal and found on poor-quality land. They tend to be unplanned and spontaneous. Houses are basic and are built using cheap materials that can be found easily, such as plastic, wood or corrugated iron. Often squatter settlements have few services.

2 As more and more people arrive in the city each day, greater pressure is placed on the city and its resources. This pressure creates a number of problems:

Overcrowding: LEDC cities often have a very high population density, particularly on the edge of the city.

Over-population: The growing populations of most LEDC cities have put pressure on services and resources such as clean water, healthcare, transport and housing.

Competition for land: Job opportunities and services tend to be poor in the squatter settlements, so migrants to the city want to live near to the CBD or good transport links. This creates competition for the best areas of land.

Disease: Poor sanitation, limited healthcare and little clean water in squatter settlements means there is a high risk of disease.

Lack of space: Settlements become dangerous if they are built on slopes at risk from mudslides, or if they are built close to factories and industrial areas.

Environmental problems: Overcrowding and a lack of resources can make it hard to dispose of waste safely and efficiently. The roads in the city can be very congested and air pollution levels very high. A lack of adequate infrastructure can mean that water pollution is also a major issue.

C Improving quality of life in LEDC cities

① key fact   A lack of money and resources means that governments and local authorities in many LEDCs are often unable to do much to reduce the problems created by rapid urbanisation.

② In the past, governments have viewed squatter settlements as a problem that must be cleared away. Many were literally bulldozed out of the way and the residents encouraged, or even forced, to go back to the countryside.

③ In recent years, governments and charities have been working with the communities that have developed in the squatter settlements to help them improve the quality of life for individuals and their families.

Site-and-service schemes give people the chance to rent or buy a piece of land that is connected to the main services of the city (e.g. water and roads). People build their own home on the land, often using money from a loan. They are encouraged to make use of their own skills and ideas to build their homes.

Self-help schemes organised by government or charities encourage the people living in shanty towns to improve their homes. Materials are supplied and loans given.

If the area improves, the residents are sometimes given legal ownership of the land. Over time, the services in the area also improve.

As well as trying to improve the quality of life in squatter settlements, governments in many LEDCs have tried to improve living conditions in rural areas. It is hoped that such schemes will discourage people from migrating to the city.

>> practice questions

1 **Give two reasons for urban growth in LEDCs.**

2 **Describe the characteristics of a squatter settlement.**

3 **Describe and explain how the quality of life for residents of a squatter settlement may be improved.**

Sustainable urban living

- There are ways in which cities can be made more sustainable.

- Sustainable urban living supports people, the economy and the environment.

- Developing sustainable cities can be a challenge.

A Sustainable cities

1 Many of the world's cities are considered unsustainable.

2 **key fact** In many places, individuals, groups and organisations are working to make cities more sustainable.

3 A sustainable city meets the needs of current residents as well as ensuring a good quality of life for future generations. A sustainable city helps support society, the economy and the environment.

- **Social sustainability** – all residents of the city have access to suitable housing and services. Local people are involved in making decisions that will affect them and others living in the city. A sense of community is important.

- **Economic sustainability** – all people have access to long-term employment opportunities, and resources are conserved for future generations. It is possible for people to get to work relatively easily and quickly, without using a car.

- **Environmental sustainability** – threats to the natural environment are managed including reducing waste, air pollution, energy use and carbon emissions. Energy is generated using renewable sources, e.g. wind. Brownfield sites are used for new housing and office developments.

4 Planning is important when developing a sustainable city. Many different interest groups are usually involved in the decision-making process. Sometimes these groups disagree; plans can change and sometimes schemes may be stopped.

5 In England there are plans to build ten eco-towns by 2020. The plans for these towns are still being approved and finalised.

6 In China, plans have been put forward to build an eco-city on the island of Chongming, Shanghai. It would be called Dongtan.

- Dongtan has been designed to promote sustainable urban living in a number of ways, including burning waste from rice paddy fields to power homes and using renewable energy sources such as hydrogen to power buses.

- However, the plans for Dongtan have been controversial; farmers could lose land and rare bird habitats could be destroyed. In 2009, development of the city stalled and little progress has been made. Politics and planning issues have been blamed.

7 The example of Dongtan shows that developing sustainable cities is a challenge.

LEDCs may find it particularly difficult to achieve sustainable urban development owing to a lack of resources. The situation is made worse because of the rapid rate of growth being experienced by most LEDC cities.

B Sustainable urban transport

1 Traffic congestion and air pollution are two of the most significant challenges facing many cities.

2 In the UK, various schemes have been introduced in an attempt to reduce the amount of traffic passing through urban areas:

Oxford Park and Ride

Park and ride schemes: People are encouraged to park their car on the edge of the town or city and travel to the CBD by bus. Such schemes have been successful in Oxford and Cambridge.

Traffic calming: To try to slow traffic down and restrict the number of cars in certain parts of the city, speed bumps have been constructed, individual roads narrowed and one-way systems introduced. This makes residential areas safer and prevents large vehicles travelling through parts of the city.

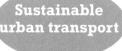
Sustainable urban transport

Light rapid transport systems (LRT): These have been introduced in many large cities, e.g. the Docklands Light Railway (DLR) in London and the Tyne and Wear Metro in Newcastle. LRT systems have fast, light trains which can travel overland and underground. The trains are automated and cheaper to run than conventional trains.

Congestion charging: Commuters are charged to enter parts of the city centre in an attempt reduce traffic at peak times. The revenue (money) generated by the scheme is used to improve public transport. London has a congestion charging zone.

Cycle networks: To try to reduce traffic congestion some cities (e.g. Cambridge) have made it safer and easier for people to use bicycles. This has been done by introducing more cycle lanes or paths, and providing places to park cycles around the city.

3 **key fact** Some schemes to reduce urban transport issues have been more successful than others. Each one has costs and benefits.

study hint >>

Make a list of the costs and benefits for each of the traffic management schemes.

>> practice questions

1 Describe the characteristics of a sustainable city.

2 What schemes can be used to reduce traffic congestion in urban areas?

3 For an urban area you have studied, describe what has been done to make it more sustainable.

Urban sprawl

- The rural–urban fringe is the point at which the city meets the countryside.

- Green belts have been established around many towns and cities to prevent urban sprawl.

- Many people are moving from cities to the countryside. This is called counter-urbanisation.

A The green belt

1. The area where the city meets the countryside is called the rural–urban fringe.

2. **key fact** MEDC cities tend to grow outwards. The spread of urban areas into the countryside is called urban sprawl.

3. In the UK, green belts have been established around many large cities to try and prevent urban sprawl. A green belt is an area of green land around the city where development is restricted and controlled. It is designed to restrict the growth of a city and to protect the countryside.

   - Conflict can arise over how the land on the green belt is used. There is growing pressure to develop areas of green-belt land.

   - Environmental groups such as the Council for the Protection of Rural England (CPRE) are against the development of green belt land.

B Counter-urbanisation

1. **key fact** The movement of people out of urban areas to live in rural areas is called counter-urbanisation. This is urban-to-rural migration.

2. Counter-urbanisation is a process happening in many MEDCs.

3. People want to live in open areas surrounded by greenery, away from the bustle and noise of urban areas. Houses tend to be cheaper in rural areas, although as the demand increases for rural homes, the price is rising.

4. Improvements in transport have made it possible for people to live in the country and commute to work in the city each day. This has led to the development of commuter villages, where many of the residents do not work in the village or surrounding area.

5. Improvements in telecommunications also make it possible for more people to work from home. This is called teleworking.

6. Counter-urbanisation has meant that the population of some inner-urban areas has declined over the last thirty to forty years.

C Consequences of counter-urbanisation

1 Counter-urbanisation can lead to a divide between newcomers to a town or village and existing residents. It may also lead to social change as people from the city bring different attitudes and values to the area.

2 Counter-urbanisation can change the population structure of an area.

- Traditionally the countryside has had a population structure skewed towards the elderly. This is because young people often move to urban areas for work and education opportunities.

- Recently, more families with children have moved into rural areas (particularly within the rural–urban fringe). This has created younger population structures (with more middle-aged residents and children).

- Rural honeypots and coastal settlements are popular areas for retirement. This creates a population structure that is mostly elderly.

3 Many village shops are being forced to close because they cannot compete with out-of-town shopping centres or large supermarkets found on the edge of towns and cities. Rural shops are not always supported by local residents, many of whom are at work during opening hours. Residents who work in an urban area tend to shop in bigger supermarkets, on the way home from work. These stores can offer a wider range of goods and services.

4 Many rural bus services are being withdrawn as most people drive to nearby towns rather than take the bus. This isolates those who cannot drive or do not have cars.

study hint >>

Remember, the fact that most people in MEDCs now own cars has changed settlement patterns including where people live and work.

Typical English village scene

>> practice questions

1 Explain why green belts were introduced around many UK cities.

2 Explain what is meant by counter-urbanisation.

3 Outline two issues caused by counter-urbanisation.

Changing farming in MEDCs

- The amount of land being farmed has decreased but it is more productive.

- To survive, farmers have had to diversify.

- Today farming works with, rather than against, the environment.

A Employment in farming

1 **key fact** Today just under 250 000 people work in agriculture compared with just over 450 000 people 30 years ago.

2 Most farming is large-scale agribusiness. Fields and farms are bigger. The latest chemicals and crop strains are used. Large machines are used in arable farming and animals are reared using factory methods.

3 The UK now imports 40% of its food from overseas as it costs less to produce.

4 Farmers get such low prices for their products and fewer subsidies from the European Union that some have gone out of business.

B Diversification

To survive, many farmers diversify. Diversification is using land for non-farming purposes. Farmers can diversify by:

- Changing their business completely. This could involve selling the land for development, barn conversions for housing or business, or industrial units.

- Continuing to farm but finding other ways to make money out of it.

Case study – Diversification at Ashlyns Farm

Ashlyns Farm is run by the Collins family and is a well-established business which farms 1500 acres of organic land near Ongar in Essex. It has moved from its mixed farming origins producing rape and wheat and rearing cattle, to running a tourist attraction and catering business as the prices of farm products have fallen. Now as well as running a working farm the Collins' make money out their land in other ways. The farm is located on the A414, 5 km from the M11 in accessible countryside. The farm now has a nature trail and education centre where schoolchildren can learn about farming. Several rare breeds are kept for visitors to handle. There is a butchers' shop and restaurant where farm produce is sold along with other locally sourced organic produce. The farm also makes its own beer in the Pittfield Brewery. It has a training centre for school cooks and was part of Jamie Oliver's School Dinners project.

C Environmental change

 Until recently, farmers have damaged the environment while trying to make a profit. Today the emphasis is on farmers working with the environment rather than against it. This is a more sustainable approach to farming.

- Organic farming does not use chemicals to kill weeds, pests, improve soil quality, or use genetically modified organisms. Instead it uses crop rotation to break pest and disease cycles and retain soil quality. It also uses green manure and compost to improve soil quality. Yields are lower but the produce commands much higher prices at market. It takes at least five years to gain organic status from the Soil Association.

- Many farmers are restoring hedgerows to their land that were ripped out in the 1960s. Re-introducing them reduces soil erosion, wind damage to crops and surface runoff. It has the benefit of providing cover and habitat for wildlife.

- Wildlife corridors are being created around the edge of fields. Difficult-to-manage corners are being left to grow wild. This is helping biodiversity as it is providing habitats for insects, rodents and bird species.

 Farmers are being helped to be environmentally friendly by the European Union, who give them grants for implementing schemes like those described above.

study hint >>

Visit or find out about a farm in your local area.

>> practice questions

1 What is diversification?

2 Explain how farmers may diversify their business.

3 How is farming today benefitting the environment?

exam tip >>

Make sure you can define major terms like 'subsidies', 'organic', 'diversify'.

Changing farming in LEDCs

- LEDCs need to increase food output to meet the needs of their rapidly growing populations.

- LEDCs need to stem the flow of people moving from their rural areas to towns and cities.

- The most successful approaches are 'grass roots' and sustainable.

A Types of farming

① key fact Most farming in LEDCs is subsistence.

② Subsistence farmers can easily fall into the property trap. Yields are low and a lack of money means that few technological advances can be introduced to improve them, so there is never money to invest in improvements. The most common types of subsistence farming are:

- Intensive arable, which uses large amounts of labour on small plots of land, such as for rice farming in the Ganges Delta.

- Intensive shifting cultivation, which uses large amounts of labour in small clearings in forests, as practiced in the Amazon Basin.

- Extensive pastoral nomadism, which uses small amounts of labour and vast amounts of land, as practised by herdsman seeking out grazing land for animals in the Sahel region of Africa.

③ key fact There is some commercial farming in LEDCs.

Most commercial farms are very large in size and are run by MEDC companies and are the legacy of a colonial past.

- Plantations use high inputs of technology and labour to produce a single crop such as rubber or bananas in places like the Caribbean. This is monoculture.

- Ranches use high inputs of technology to clear land and raise animals for meat products in places like Brazil.

B Changes in farming

① key fact In many LEDCs, farming yields have not increased at the same rate as the country's population over the last fifty years.

② key fact Since the 1960s, many LEDC farmers have tried to match food production to demand by using high-yield crops. This was called the Green Revolution.

Many people in LEDCs now feel that MEDC farming methods do not always work for them as they are not always successful economically or environmentally.

3 New approaches aim to increase production to achieve food security but in a sustainable way and to improve living conditions and poverty in rural areas to stop people moving away. In practical terms this means:

- developing simple equipment which can be easily maintained

- using affordable local labour, skills and materials so farmers do not go into debt

- using farming methods that use natural fertilisers and do not harm the land

- improving transport so farmers have better access to local markets

- introducing clean water

- giving people better access to healthcare and education

- connecting to the national electricity grid or providing solar alternatives

- giving villages access to the internet and mobile phones to reduce remoteness.

study hint >>

Food security means access to sufficient and affordable food at a household or global level.

4 Improvements are delivered at grass roots level by NGOs such as Christian Aid to help LEDC rural areas achieve their Millennium Development Goals. In Mali they support small-scale farmers to adapt to the changing environment and develop green energy, creating new ways for people living far from the capital, Bamako, and the national grid, to earn a living.

Case study – Millennium promise in Malawi

This NGO uses simple technology to improve food security and quality of life in Mwandama by:

- Giving farmers access to markets by improving a 5 km stretch of road and building two bridges over rivers.
- Providing 200 solar-powered lanterns for reading and working in homes to help small business enterprises and education.
- Providing outreach clinics to treat malaria to enable children to attend school more regularly and adults to work more productively.
- Providing maize seeds and green fertilisers at cheap rates. This has increased production by 1100%.
- Encouraging people to diversify into higher-value products such as fruit, vegetables and honey.

>> practice questions

1 **What types of farming are there in LEDCs?**

2 **Why do LEDCs need to increase food production?**

3 **How are LEDC rural areas developing sustainably?**

exam tip >>

Top answers will describe the use of schemes in detail and explain how they are sustainable economically and environmentally.

Globalisation

A Globalisation

1 Globalisation is a term used to describe the way in which people and places are becoming increasingly connected.

2 **key fact** People are becoming more and more connected due to developments in transport and communications technology.

3 Globalisation has changed many areas of modern life.

Cultural changes – people can now take part in and enjoy each other's cultures; for example, restaurants from around the world are found in many towns and cities in the UK. People can also watch television programmes and films from around the world.

Economic changes – many places in the world are highly connected to each other via networks of trade. The latest technology means that goods and services can be traded between countries far more easily. The parts for a product may be manufactured in one country and then assembled in another.

Political changes – technology such as the internet allows people to find out about what is going on in the world very quickly and relatively easily. This means that political campaigns can gather support from people all over the world. Many countries in the world are members of international groups, e.g. the G20 and have signed up to international agreements such as the Antarctic Treaty.

Changes brought about by globalisation

Demographic changes (changes in population) – as travel has become easier and trade between countries has continued to develop, migration has become a big part of globalisation. Economic migrants may often move abroad for work. Some areas of the world now have fewer border controls, which makes international migration easier, e.g. the European Union. (See page 102 on Migration.)

Lifestyle changes – globalisation has made travel much easier and quicker. This means that people can visit places around the world relatively easily. People can also buy products made in countries all around the world.

4 **key fact** Globalisation is not entirely new. Connections and networks of trade between countries have existed for a long time. What has changed is the speed at which we are globalising and the depth of our connections. This is mainly due to developments in technology.

B The impacts of globalisation

1 **key fact** Not everyone benefits from globalisation; there are winners and losers.

exam tip >>

When talking about the impacts of something in an exam, make sure you give a balanced argument that includes both positive and negative impacts.

2 Globalisation has enabled people to travel the world and provided them with a vast range of products to buy.

- However, the connections that have bought people across the world closer together are not experienced by everyone; some countries are more connected than others.

- Some people do not have access to the latest communications and travel technology. Some countries do not trade extensively with others.

3 Although most countries are connected through trade, this trade doesn't always take place on equal terms. For example, some LEDCs trade only in primary products, e.g. bananas. These products are sold at a low price. The growers are not likely to receive a very large share of any profits that are made. (See page 106 on fair trade.)

4 Globalisation can have environmental impacts. For example, transport technology can emit harmful pollutants into the atmosphere. The extraction of resources and the production of goods can also harm the natural environment.

5 Some people feel so strongly about the negative impacts of globalisation that they protest against it. For example, there were protests during the 2009 G20 Summit held in London.

C Transnational corporations (TNCs)

1 TNCs are companies that operate across the world, in many nations. Coca-Cola and Nike are well-known TNCs. Such companies are sometimes called multinational corporations (MNCs).

2 TNCs design, produce and market goods on a global scale.

3 TNCs will source materials from and make goods in the cheapest locations in the world to maximise profits. TNCs tend to have their headquarters in MEDCs and their production centres in LEDCs.

4 TNCs are important agents of globalisation. 40% of the world's trade is carried out by the 350 largest TNCs.

study hint >>

You may have studied an example TNC. Make sure you know how it operates and the impacts it has had on different places.

5 TNCs can bring both opportunities and challenges to a place. For example, TNCs can provide jobs and boost local economies. However, they can be accused of exploiting workers and harming local environments.

>> practice questions

1 Explain how developments in transport and communications technology have created a more globalised world.

2 What are the impacts of globalisation?

3 How do TNCs contribute to the process of globalisation?

The global economy

- International trade between countries has created a global economy.

- Trade and industry are key parts of the global economy.

- There are four main sectors of industry: primary, secondary, tertiary and quaternary.

- The structure of a country's industry depends on its level of development.

A The global economy

>> **key fact** The global economy is a system of trade involving countries from around the world.

- Globalisation has been a powerful force in shaping the global economy.

- Trade, industry and business are key parts of the global economy.

B Industry

remember >>
The four sectors of industry are connected.

1. Industry is any economic activity that involves collecting raw materials, producing goods and providing services.

2. **key fact** There are four main sectors of industry.

Primary industry collects raw materials by growing, catching or extraction. The main industries include fishing, forestry, mining and quarrying.
A primary job would be a miner extracting bauxite.

Tertiary industry provides services.
The main industries include retailing, education, healthcare, administration and transport.
A tertiary job would be a salesperson selling a car in a showroom.

Secondary industry processes raw materials and assembles a finished product. The main industries include metal making, assembling machines and vehicles and construction.
A secondary job would be a foundry worker processing bauxite into aluminium and a factory worker assembling the aluminium in a car body.

Industrial sectors

Quaternary industry researches and develops new products or provides new services. The main industries include marketing, advertising, telecommunications, biotechnology and information technology.
A quaternary job would be a design engineer researching and developing new car models.

C Employment structure

1 **key fact** Employment is the job people do in a specific industry.

2 Employment structure is the percentage of workers employed in each sector of industry, in a given area. It can be shown as:

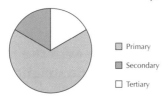

- Primary
- Secondary
- Tertiary

A pie chart for country A

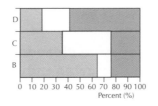

A divided bar graph

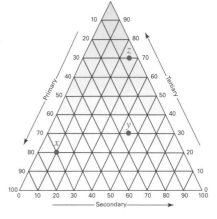

A triangular graph

3 Employment structure varies between countries. It is often influenced by a country's level of development.

- MEDCs tend to have a high percentage employed in tertiary industry.
- LEDCs tend to have a high percentage employed in primary industry.

4 Employment structure also varies in a country over time.

- **Pre-industrialisation**: a high percentage work in primary industry.
- **Industrialisation**: a significant percentage work in secondary industry.
- **Deindustrialisation**: a high percentage work in tertiary and quaternary industries. The UK is now in this phase.

D The location of industry

1 **key fact** The location of industry is influenced by a combination of factors:

Transport costs	Capital	Fuel supply	Deicision-makers	Linked industries	Labour supply
Globalisation	Technological change	Proximity to markets	Raw materials	Agglomeration economics	Government change

2 Once a general area has been chosen for an industry, the exact location must be found. Local site factors, such as the size of the site, transport links, accessibility and cost, become important.

3 Many modern industries are footloose. This means that they can locate almost anywhere and they can relocate easily if they need to.

>> practice questions

1 List two examples of each for primary, secondary and tertiary industry jobs.

2 What is the employment structure for countries x, y and z using the triangular graph above?

3 What factors may a company have to take into account when deciding where to locate a factory?

Changing industry in MEDCs

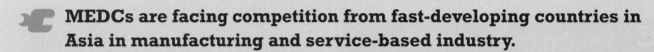

- **MEDCs are facing competition from fast-developing countries in Asia in manufacturing and service-based industry.**

- **MEDCs are developing high-value knowledge-based industries.**

A Manufacturing industry

1. **key fact** Many factories have closed in Western Europe over the last 20 years. This decline in manufacturing industry is called deindustrialisation.

2. At a global level, the location of manufacturing industry has shifted from MEDCs to newly industrialised countries (NICs) and LEDCs.

3. Today around 20% of the UK's workforce are employed in manufacturing compared with about 40% in the 1960s. This has happened because:

   - Machines can do the jobs of people.
   - The price of goods made in the UK is too high in the global marketplace.
   - There is a good availability of cheap labour in LEDCs.
   - It is relatively cheap and quick to transport manufactured goods from factories in LEDCs to major world markets.
   - Information can be transferred quickly by the internet.
   - TNCs have grown.

4. The movement of manufacturing industry has brought costs and benefits to LEDCs and NICs.

5. Deindustrialisation has had a negative economic and social impact on traditional manufacturing areas in MEDCs. However, regeneration schemes can improve the landscape and economy of former industrial areas (see pages 84–5 on urban regeneration).

B Tertiary industry

1. **key fact** While secondary industry has declined, tertiary industry has grown and the UK has attracted high-technology manufacturing industry to invest here.

2. **key fact** Tertiary industry, which provides services such as banking, finance, insurance, retailing and leisure, is the most important sector of the UK economy. Around 70% of people work in these areas.

   - This area of work has grown as with increased population and wealth there is a greater demand for more goods and services, which creates more jobs and spending on basic and luxury items.
   - Improved technology allows new services to develop such as gaming and website design.
   - In addition, as the UK has developed it has improved health and education services which are major employers.

3 High-technology industry involves making electronic equipment such as computers, software or other high-value goods. As they use light raw materials and power from the national grid, these industries can choose where to locate. Footloose industries like this are often found on the edges of towns and cities in science and business parks and on industrial estates. The companies often group together in a cluster (e.g. Cambridge Science Park) because they benefit from being close to each other.

Cambridge Science Park

4 **key fact** However, some functions within service industries are facing the same pressures from overseas as manufacturing industry, as labour accounts for about 70% of total costs.

Customer services are outsourcing to lower-wage locations such as Bangalore in India for BT Broadband Support and the Philippines for HSBC telephone banking.

C The changing workplace

study hint >>

Create your own media file of relevant newspaper articles.

1 **key fact** There is a move away from secondary and tertiary industry (the production of goods and services) towards a knowledge-based economy (the quaternary sector).

This employs people in research and development and consultancy and is reliant on technology.

2 Because of the growth of wireless networks and the internet, people can now work anywhere and at any time.

This has led to the growth of flexible working patterns such as teleworking (working from home), job sharing, part-time working and flexi-working. This has allowed women to enter and remain in the workforce in greater numbers.

3 **key fact** As the population in MEDCs continues to age, workers are getting older and are required to work until an older age, at least 65.

- As society ages, the total number of people available to work declines and the skill set changes.
- All sectors of the economy will need migrant workers to plug job and skills shortages as well as contribute to the economy.

>> practice questions

1 Outline the main causes of deindustrialisation.

2 What is footloose industry?

3 Why has manufacturing industry declined in the UK?

exam tip >>

Learn the meanings of key terms like 'deindustrialisation', 'high technology' and 'outsourcing'.

Changing industry in LEDCs

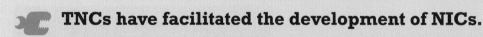

- TNCs have facilitated the development of NICs.

- Many people in NICs have benefitted from improved living standards.

- Industrialisation has also caused environmental pollution.

A Achieving industrialisation

1 key fact Some LEDC governments have successfully exploited their large populations (which provide plentiful supplies of cheap labour and large domestic markets) and industrialised their societies.

- These are now known as newly industrialising countries or NICs.
- Early NICs were concentrated in South America (Brazil, Mexico) and South East Asia.

2 key fact New NICs continue to develop around the Pacific Rim. They include Thailand, Malaysia, Philippines, Indonesia and China.

Early NICs
New NICs

3 Most NICs have taken the same series of steps to achieve their aims.

Becoming an NIC

Borrow to develop infrastructure and educate. Th attracts TNCs to the country.

→

Use income and skills from TNCs to develop own high-value consumer goods.

→

Import restrictions (to protect domestic markets) devalue currency, making exports cheaper.

Reliance on MEDC TNCs decreases as they seek new markets elsewhere. Industrialisation and NIC status achieved.

←

Further investment in infrastructure and own companies – some become TNCs like LG in South Korea. Living standards improve rapidly, but so do production costs.

B Impacts of industrialisation

Industrialisation has both costs and benefits for NICs.

Benefits ✔	Costs ✖
• Speeds the development process	• Profits 'leak' back to MEDCs
• Creates large-scale employment in the formal sector	• Much employment is low paid and unskilled
• Linked industries develop	• Often poor working conditions
• Skills transfer to host country	• Factories pollute the environment. They can cause air pollution and water pollution. Chemicals and waste from factories may be dumped in rivers.
• Leads to increased investment from outside	• Jobs in cities encourage migration to the city, so fewer people to produce food
• Exports rise, generating income and investment	• LEDCs remain vulnerable if TNCs pull out due to dropping demand for the product or can locate elsewhere more economically.
• Increased living standards, reducing poverty	• MEDC values and consumer culture become dominant at the expense of traditional spiritual values.

C Will all LEDCs become NICs?

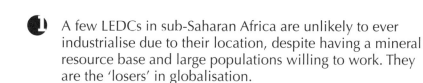

1 A few LEDCs in sub-Saharan Africa are unlikely to ever industrialise due to their location, despite having a mineral resource base and large populations willing to work. They are the 'losers' in globalisation.

- The majority of the secondary workforce remain in the informal sector which caters for local, not global, markets.

- Output and profits are low, leaving little money to invest in improvements.

- The infrastructure is underdeveloped, transport is poor and power supplies unreliable.

- There are too few skilled workers.

- Global trading patterns favour MEDCs.

- TNCs are unwilling to invest in unstable countries.

> **exam tip >>**
>
> **Be able to describe the distribution of NICs.**

>> practice questions

1 Why do some LEDCs find it hard to industrialise?

2 What is an NIC?

3 What steps do NICs take to protect their own developing industries?

4 Describe the social impacts of industrialisation on NICs.

Measuring global differences in developmen

- Levels of development and quality of life vary between countries.
- Different indicators can be used to measure a country's development.
- In 2000, the United Nations set eight goals aimed at eradicating extreme world poverty by 2015.

A An unequal world

1 **key fact** Globally there are vast differences in quality of life.

2 **key fact** Some countries are more developed than others.

- Wealthier countries with high standards of living are often called more economically developed countries (MEDCs).

- Poorer countries with generally low standards of living are often called less economically developed countries (LEDCs).

- It is important to understand that differences exist within countries as well as between them.

- Human development involves making economic progress in a country and raising living standards (this includes making improvements to health, education and housing).

B How can we measure development?

1 Deciding how developed a country is can be difficult. Different criteria can be used to measure development. These are called indicators of development.

2 In the past, a country's level of development was measured by assessing its wealth. This was done by calculating a country's Gross National Product (GNP), which is the amount of wealth produced through trade, services and industry in one year. GNP figures were given in US dollars and calculated per person.

3 Recently, governments and international organisations have begun using a wide range of indicators to measure development, including social and political criteria:

- **average life expectancy**: how long the average person in a country is expected to live

- **infant mortality**: how many babies die before their first birthday

- **adult literacy**: the number of adults who can read and write

- **access to clean water**: the percentage of the population with access to it

- **calorie intake**: the average number of calories eaten per day

- **access to healthcare**: the number of patients per doctor

- **women's rights**: the percentage of women in government.

remember >>

Development in a country is not just about money. Social and political conditions are also very important.

(4) The United Nations measures development using the Human Development Index (HDI).

- The HDI uses a range of indicators to assess a country's development including life expectancy, literacy, GDP and educational attainment.

- Countries are given a score and then ranked. In 2008 Iceland was ranked top of the development index. Sierra Leone was placed at the bottom.

- The HDI is also split into three categories: high, medium and low human development.

C The Millennium Development Goals

(1) The gap between the most advanced and least advanced countries in the world is known as the development gap. Some people argue that this gap is growing.

study hint >>

All countries are different; try not to generalise too much about places.

(2) To try to close the development gap the United Nations has drawn up a set of targets that it hopes will help eradicate extreme world poverty by 2015.

- These targets are called the Millennium Development Goals (MDGs).

- Over 180 countries have agreed to meet these goals.

- There are eight Millennium Development Goals:

End hunger	Reduce those suffering from hunger and poverty by half.
Universal education	Ensure that all boys and girls complete a full course of primary schooling.
Gender equality	Eliminate gender disparity in primary and secondary education.
Child health	Reduce by two-thirds the mortality rate of children under five.
Maternal health	Reduce by three-quarters the maternal mortality rate.
Combat HIV/Aids	Halt and begin to reverse the spread of HIV/Aids and other diseases.
Environmental sustainability	Integrate the principles of sustainable development into country policies and programmes.
Global partnership	Develop open trading and financial systems that are non-discriminatory.

(3) Since the MDGs were set, some countries have made very good progress and are on track to meet their targets by 2015 (e.g. China). There is concern that many countries in sub-Saharan Africa will fail to meet their targets.

>> practice questions

1 **Describe three ways in which development can be measured.**

2 **Explain how the Millennium Development Goals are being used to reduce poverty and inequality.**

exam tip >>

When writing exam answers try to use terms like 'generally', 'mostly' and 'tend to'.

Trade, aid and development

- The world trade system favours MEDCs.

- Poor terms of trade and donations of aid can make LEDCs dependent on MEDCs.

- Many people believe that progress is made through fair trade and schemes that promote sustainable development.

A Development through trade

1 **key fact** Many LEDCs have tried to develop their economies through international trade.

2 Trade involves the exchange of goods and services within and between countries. Trade between countries is called international trade. Importing goods involves buying goods from other countries. Exporting goods involves selling goods to other countries. The difference between the value of imports and exports is known as the balance of trade.

3 The pattern of world trade is uneven. LEDCs have a small share of world trade compared to MEDCs. Over 80 per cent of world trade involves MEDCs.

4 Traditionally, most LEDCs have traded with MEDCs by exporting primary goods and importing manufactured goods. This system of trade favours MEDCs and can cause problems for LEDCs.

remember >>

LEDCs are often disadvantaged by the world trade system. MEDCs tend to benefit from international trade, LEDCs often lose out.

Primary goods, such as crops (sugar, coffee), are low-value products and do not make large profits for LEDCs. The value of primary goods can fluctuate a great deal on the world market and LEDCs are not guaranteed a price for their products.

Manufactured goods are high-value products. MEDCs make a profit selling them.

LEDCs spend more importing manufactured goods than they make selling primary goods. This gives LEDCs a **poor balance of trade**.

MEDCs can buy primary products at a low cost from LEDCs and export manufactured goods at a profit. MEDCs have a **good balance of trade**.

B Fair trade

1 Fair trade involves making sure that companies and workers in LEDCs are paid a good price for the goods they produce.

2 Retailers (sellers) in MEDCs buy raw materials and manufactured goods from LEDCs at a guaranteed price and sell them to consumers. The retailer then makes sure that a good share of the profits are returned to LEDCs.

3 Fair trade is a growing area of business in MEDCs. Many large food stores now sell fair-trade items. More and more product labels give information about the origin of different foodstuffs and the conditions of the workers.

C Development through aid

1 **key fact** Many LEDCs rely upon aid to help them with economic and social development.

2 There are different types of development aid:

Non-governmental aid: Provided by charities and independent organisations (e.g. Oxfam). It's not directed by governments and often relies on fundraisers and volunteers. Non-governmental organisations (NGOs) tend to support small-scale local development projects (e.g. running health clinics or building a freshwater well).

Multilateral aid: Donated by several different countries, usually through an international agency or organisation (e.g. the UN or World Bank).

The three main types of aid

Bilateral aid: Given directly from the government of one country to another. Includes donations of money, food, technology or training services.

3 One of the biggest concerns about using aid for development in LEDCs is making sure that the aid given to poorer countries is appropriate to their needs and reaches the people who need it most.

D Development projects

1 In the past many LEDCs used large development projects to try to generate income and improve their country's infrastructure (e.g. roads, railways, electricity and water supply).

- Such projects may involve building a dam, e.g. the Three Gorges Dam in China, or road construction, e.g. the Trans Amazonian highway.

- The use of large-scale projects is called 'top-down' development. The hope is that the money invested in the scheme and its benefits will trickle down to other areas of the country or region.

2 Large development projects tend to rely upon heavy foreign investment and aid.

- During the 1970s and 1980s many LEDCs took out loans from MEDCs and the World Bank for development projects. Unfortunately, during the 1980s interest rates rose rapidly and LEDCs are now left with large debts that they can't repay.

- In recent years, large development projects have become unpopular with some governments, charities and international organisations. Some projects have failed to improve the quality of life for poor communities and there have been concerns about corruption.

3 Today many people favour small-scale, 'bottom-up' development projects. They hope that these will bring about long-term changes for an area.

- Small-scale development is sometimes called grass roots development. It involves making small changes to an area, working with local people and using local skills.

- Non-governmental organisations (NGOs) often provide training and education to help communities with grass roots projects.

4 **key fact** Small-scale development projects aim to be sustainable and appropriate to the needs of local people.

>> practice questions

1 Explain why LEDCs tend to have a poor balance of trade.

2 Why are some LEDCs dependent on MEDCs for trade and aid?

3 How can fair trade help LEDCs to develop?

Tourism

 Tourism is a service industry.

 Tourism is the world's fastest growing industry, employing roughly 10% of the global workforce.

 Tourism has positive and negative impacts on people and places.

A Tourism as an industry

 ① **key fact** Tourism is an activity that involves a visit away from home.

- A tourist is someone who spends at least one night away from their normal place of residence.
- The visit may be a holiday or it could be business travel, visiting friends and relatives, a religious pilgrimage or a trip to gain health treatment.

② Tourism is a worldwide industry employing roughly 10% of all people of working age.

Globally, 903 million international visits were made by tourists in 2007.

③ **key fact** Tourism has been the world's fastest growing industry since the 1950s.

People are taking more holidays, for longer, and spending more of their disposable income on them.

> **remember >>**
> Tourism is the world's fastest growing industry.

Changing transport
Improved roads and increased car ownership, introduction of large jet aircraft, more airports.

Changing costs
Travel companies offer cheap, organised package holidays, airlines offer 'no frills' and discounted fares.

Changing attitudes
Public exposed to exotic locations in the media, people now expect to have at least one holiday a year, the active elderly have the time and money to spend on travel, people expect excitement and adventure from holidays.

Reasons for the growth in tourism

Changing work patterns
Fewer hours worked so more leisure time, more flexible hours, paid holiday, longer periods of holiday leave, increased wages relative to inflation.

B Classifying tourism

① **key fact** Tourism is often referred to as a resource-based industry. It depends on a combination of primary and secondary resources.

- **Primary resources** occur naturally:

  Attractive climates (sun/snow)

  Landforms (beaches/mountains/lakes)

  Ecosystems/wildlife

- **Secondary resources** are man-made:

  Infrastructure (accommodation/transport)

  Attractions (monuments/religious/stately

  homes/industrial/historic/heritage sites)

  Entertainment (sporting events/culture/

  shopping/theme parks)

Lake Hawea, New Zealand

2 Tourism can also be classified by:

- **Location** (seaside/countryside/urban)
- **Activity** (passive/active)
- **Duration** (length of visit)
- **Distance** travelled (local/international).

C The impacts of tourism

New Globe Theatre, London

1 **key fact** **Both MEDCs and LEDCs want to develop tourist industries because of the wealth it can generate.**

However, there are often hidden costs:

	Benefits ✔	Costs ✖
Economic	Employment; foreign exchange	Jobs are often low-paid, of low status and temporary
Socio-cultural	Local cultures and traditions maintained	Local culture and traditions exploited
Environmental	Fragile sites and landforms can be protected	Fragile ecosystems often permanently damaged

2 In order to reduce the impact of tourism, many companies and organisations have tried to make tourism a more sustainable industry.

Eco-tourism and community tourism are forms of sustainable tourism.

exam tip **>>**

Questions will ask you to discuss the costs as well as the benefits of tourism.

>> practice questions

1 **What factors have led to a growth in the tourism industry?**

2 **Describe three ways in which tourism can be classified.**

3 **What social, economic and environmental impacts might tourism have on a country?**

Rural tourism in the UK

- **More and more people are visiting the countryside in the UK.**
- **Visitors often visit national parks.**
- **Tourism has both positive and negative impacts on national parks.**

A Changing UK tourism

1 **key fact** **Early tourism in the UK was based on coastal resorts.**

- This form of tourism began in the 1700s when the elite visited spas and early seaside resorts. Mass tourism developed in the UK in the 1800s when railway connections took people from major cities to seaside towns like Bournemouth and Blackpool. The heyday of bucket-and-spade holidays was in the 1950s. However, in the 1970s competition from southern Europe (particularly Spain) and air travel meant that many holidaymakers started to go abroad. Some resorts have gone into decline, while others (e.g. Brighton) have rebranded and remain very popular.

- British coastal resorts have followed similar trends to that shown in the Butler model which shows growth and decline cycles in tourist destinations.

2 Today rural areas are very popular destinations in the UK.

A lot of rural tourism involves visits to national parks and scenic upland areas.

B National parks

1 **key fact** **National parks are large areas of relatively unspoilt scenic countryside protected for use by the public now and in the future.**

2 **key fact** **It is estimated that over 110 million people visit the national parks of England and Wales each year.**

3 Ten national parks were established in England and Wales in 1950. By 2009 there were 13 national parks in England and Wales, covering a total of 5648 sq miles (14,459 sq km) of countryside:

- Northumberland
- Brecon Beacons
- New Forest
- South Downs
- Lake District
- Pembrokeshire Coast
- Norfolk Broads
- Peak District
- Dartmoor
- Yorkshire Dales
- Snowdonia
- Exmoor
- North York Moors

4 The aim of national parks is to give the public access to attractive environments while preserving the landscape and looking after the interests of local people and businesses.

5 Conflicts between different interest groups is common in most national parks.

remember >>

It is important to be able to locate each National Park on a map of the UK.

Facts and location

- Located to the north and west of Leeds and east of Lancashire
- Within 120 minutes driving distance of nine million people
- Approximately 70 km wide and 60 km deep at its widest points
- Each year over eight million people visit the park. Most travel by car.
- Eighteen thousand people live within the national park boundary.

Attractions

- Upland area of spectacular limestone scenery
- Beautiful wooded valleys and waterfalls
- Historic villages and monuments
- Adventure activities: rock climbing, potholing

Issues

- Local residents, farmers and businesses sometimes conflict with tourist use of the area, but tourism provides the main source of income for local people.
- Overcrowding happens when visitors converge on honeypots, such as Malham village. A 'honeypot' is a site that is the focus of tourist activity in an area.
- Ninety per cent of visitors come by car, congesting roads, reducing air quality, causing noise pollution; car parks are visually intrusive in the landscape and overspill at peak times.
- Visitors erode footpaths and create gullies when vegetation-cover is trampled, leaving ugly scars on hillsides. Visitors create litter, leave gates open and worry animals.
- The sheer volume of visitors has changed the character of Malham, which is now dominated by tourist facilities. This reduces the number of essential services available to residents.

- Locals are pushed out as city-dwellers buy second homes for occasional use at prices locals can't afford. Out of season, the park seems dead.
- Local limestone quarries provide local jobs but spoil the view for tourists.

Making the park sustainable

- A balance must be struck between the needs of visitors and the needs of local people and businesses.
- Improving public-transport links to the parks, so people leave their cars at home.
- Locating car parks wisely, screening them from view and using local materials for the surface.
- Rebuilding footpaths to limit erosion, replant in badly eroded areas, limit public access during wet periods when erosion is worst.
- Restricting development to honeypots to keep other villages and beauty spots pristine.
- Providing affordable housing for locals.

>> practice questions

1 **Why did some UK coastal resorts need to rebrand in the 1970s and 1980s?**

2 **What is a national park?**

3 **What conflicts exist between different interest groups in Yorkshire Dales National Park?**

4 **How is the Yorkshire Dales National Park managed?**

exam tip >>

Learn as many facts and figures about your case studies as you can.

Tourism issues in LEDCs

 LEDCs are now popular tourist destinations.

 Tourism plays an important part in helping LEDCs to develop.

 LEDCs are constantly striving to achieve a balance between the development and exploitation of their tourist resources.

A Tourism and development

 ① key fact **Tourism has become a global industry.**

- The world is shrinking due to shorter flying times. Cheaper travel has opened up far-away locations in LEDCs for the ordinary traveller.
- Many LEDCs are attractive destinations.

| Year-round hot climates | | Relatively cheap holidays |

| Different cultures to experience | | Beautiful beaches and scenery |

Kandy, Sri Lanka

- Popular destinations include Thailand, Mexico, Sri Lanka and Kenya.

 ② LEDCs are keen to promote their attractions, as tourism helps to fund development of new facilities.

 ③ The benefits of tourism to LEDCs are mostly economic.

The benefits of tourism	The costs of tourism
• Increased wealth and investment in the area (often from TNCs or companies based in MEDCs) • Foreign exchange is generated • Income from tourism can be spent on improving infrastructure and services, e.g. transport and health care. • New job opportunities are created • The multiplier effect is set in motion (this means that jobs are created in local businesses that supply the tourism industry, e.g. souvenirs and catering).	• LEDCs may go into debt in order to develop their tourism infrastructure. • Many jobs are seasonal with low status and low pay. • Many of the profits 'leak' back to the headquarters of TNCs (found in MEDCs). • Mass tourism often exploits and harms local traditions and cultures. • Large-scale damage can be caused to fragile environments and ecosystems, e.g. beaches and coral reefs. Pressure is also placed upon water supplies.

B Sustainable tourism

1 **key fact** Sustainable tourism is tourism that uses resources in a way that benefits people both now and in the future. The area benefits from tourism but without harming the environment or the local way of life.

2 Environmentally friendly, low-impact, low-density tourism is an alternative to mass tourism in most LEDCs. It is a less damaging way to develop tourism.

Ecotourism involves tourists visiting important and attractive natural environments. They learn about the area and the wildlife and how to protect it.

3 The main aims of ecotourism are to:

- protect the natural environment

- enable local people to earn money

- enable the community itself to improve local infrastructure and facilities

- enable the local community to choose how their tourism industry develops.

Ecotourism encourages tourists to explore LEDC tourist areas in small groups, staying in local accommodation, eating local food and observing local customs and culture. These holidays are expensive and try to help conserve the local environment. Most of the money is returned to the local economy. Countries that have developed ecotourism successfully include Costa Rica and Botswana.

4 **key fact** As the projects are small-scale, damage to the LEDC is minimal, but as the destination increases in popularity, it becomes more difficult to operate in a sustainable way.

Often the lure of large amounts of foreign exchange from MEDCs is too great and there is not enough expertise within the LEDC itself to protect and manage its own tourist industry appropriately.

remember >>

LEDCs are seeking a balance between development and exploitation.

>> practice questions

1 Why are LEDCs attractive destinations?

2 Explain the multiplier effect.

3 What is sustainable tourism?

4 List three benefits and three costs of tourism to LEDCs.

exam tip >>

You need to be able to discuss the economic, social and environmental impacts of tourism in LEDCs.

Case study
Tourism in the Costa del Sol, Spain

 Mass tourism has developed along the Mediterranean coastline of Spain.

 Tourism developed because of abundant resources and cheap package holidays.

A Facts and figures

>> **key fact** In just over forty years, Spain has transformed its Mediterranean coastline from a string of sleepy fishing villages to a series of international coastal resorts.

- The Costa del Sol is located in the south of Spain on the Mediterranean.

- The number of visitors to the area has soared from 0.4 million in 1960 to approximately 15.7 million in 2008.

- Before the 1960s, most jobs were in farming or fishing and the infrastructure was poor. Living standards were low, and migration of the young, high. The region was underdeveloped.

- Tourism boomed in the 1970s and 1980s. Resorts developed along the coast.

- By the late 1990s Spanish resorts were in decline; less developed, more exotic locations became available to tourists.

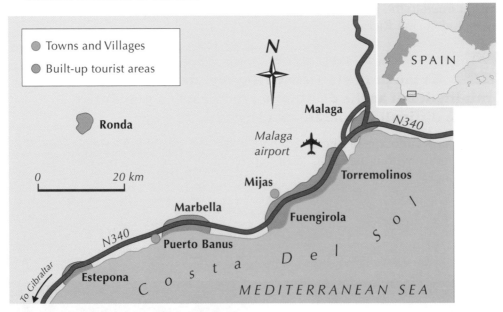

B Tourist resources

1 **Natural resources** – dry, warm climate from May to November, long sandy beaches, rugged mountains

2 **Man-made resources** – historic and cultural towns, well-developed infrastructure, wide variety of entertainment and nightlife

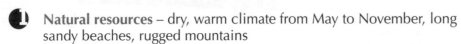

remember >>

Link tourism on the Costa del Sol to the Butler model (the tourism life cycle).

C Impacts of tourism

The impact of development along this stretch of coast has been both positive and negative.

	Benefits ✔	Costs ✖
Economic	• Improved infrastructure (upgrade of electricity supplies, Malaga airport and by-pass) • Improved employment prospects and living standards • Over 70% of people now work in tourism.	• Most employment is irregular, low-paid and of low status. • Unemployment in the region has risen and many businesses have closed down. • Falling house prices • Over-reliance on a single industry causes problems when visitor numbers fall in economic downturns.
Sociocultural	• Traditional crafts (e.g. lace-making) and industries have been saved from dying out as goods are sold as souvenirs. • Close-knit communities have stayed intact, cultural traditions (e.g. dances) retained	• Traditional lifestyles based around the church and family eroded, traditions kept artificially alive, local culture debased into tourist shows • Increased crime (drugs, vandalism and mugging)
Environmental	• Some areas protected due to investment from tourist revenue • Some beaches have EU Blue Flag status. • Nature reserves set up	• High-rise accommodation creates visual pollution. Some 1960s hotels look run-down. • Traffic congestion in towns • Litter on beaches, sea polluted with sewage from tourist waste • Pressure on local water supplies in a region with little rainfall

D The way ahead

 Due to a poor media image, tourists began turning their backs on Spain in the 1990s as cheaper LEDC holidays became more available.

 Steps have been taken to rejuvenate the Costa del Sol to attract visitors back all year round.

• Further high-rise development banned. Any new building must be low-rise and in a traditional Spanish courtyard style. Resorts such as Marbella promoted as up-market

• Resort centres pedestrianised and planted with trees, marinas and by-passes built

• Development restricted to golf courses and luxury villas between resorts

exam tip >>

You should be able to draw a labelled location map for this case study.

>> practice questions

1 What are the effects of tourism along the Costa del Sol?

2 How is the region responding to competition?

Case study
Tourism in Kenya

> ✂ **Most tourism in Kenya has developed along the Indian Ocean coast and in the game parks.**
>
> ✂ **Tourism has brought economic benefits but also social and environmental costs.**

A Facts and figures

1 Kenya is on the east coast of Africa and was one of the first LEDCs to develop mass tourism in the 1970s. It is English-speaking (due to past colonial links) and most visitors come from the UK and northern Europe.

2 **key fact** In 2008 over $870 million was earned from tourism. In terms of foreign exchange earnings, tourism is the third largest source of income for Kenya after horticulture and tea exports.

> **remember >>**
> Kenya is at the rejuvenate or decline stage of the tourism life cycle.

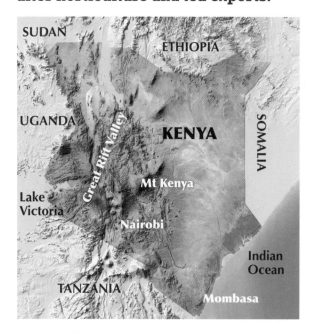

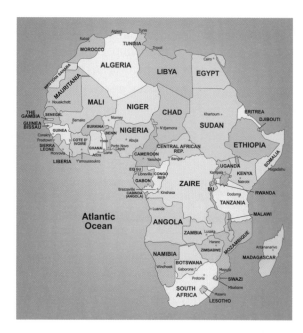

B Tourist resources

1 **Natural resources** – year-round hot climate, sandy beaches, coral reefs, wildlife reserves

2 **Man-made resources** – relatively well-developed infrastructure due to colonial links and interesting diversity of cultures such as the Masai Mara.

3 Most tourists mix a beach holiday at Malindi or Mombassa with a short safari on a game reserve.

African elephant

Impacts of tourism

The concentration of tourists in environmentally sensitive areas in Kenya has had a largely negative impact on the people and the environment.

	Benefits	Costs ✖
Economic	• 500 000+ employed in tourism • Improved living standards • Foreign exchange allows some development of the infrastructure. • Masai can sell firewood to lodges.	• Jobs are often temporary and low-paid. • Foreign TNCs own 80% of hotels and travel companies in Kenya, so profits leak back to MEDCs.
Sociocultural	• Masai settlements used as tourist attractions • Traditional culture and skills retained	• Nomadic communities displaced when reserves set up. Loss of dignity and traditional ways • Alcohol and western flesh offend Muslim coastal communities. • Sex tourism exploits the poor.
Environmental	• The exploitation of a few areas protects the majority of habitats and wildlife. • Profits from tourism can be invested in protecting other environments for the future. • Reserves allow endangered species to thrive.	• Coral reef damaged by people and boats, local fishermen can't use the seas as the ecosystem is destroyed • Overuse and inappropriate development of the shoreline • Game park minibuses churn up the bush, create soil erosion, altering the animals' behaviour • Balloon safaris frighten animals. • Savannah hotels/campsites use limited freshwater and wood.

The way ahead

 Due to tourist harassment, the risk from terrorism, over-commercialisation of safaris, destruction of natural resources, and post-election violence, visitor numbers dropped by 40% in 2008.

The Kenyan government is now acting to protect Kenya's tourist industry by limiting the use of existing marine and game parks and taxing tourists and holiday companies who use them. It is also encouraging:

- **Sustainable tourism on safari.** The Tsavo Game Park has temporary camps, limited power supplies and trails in small groups that employ local people.

- **Sustainable coastal tourism.** At Lamu, visitors pay a local tax, stay in small guesthouses and observe local customs. There's no development above tree height.

study hint >>

Look at travel brochures to familiarise yourself with typical holidays to Kenya.

>> practice questions

1 **What tourist resources does Kenya offer?**

2 **How can tourism be environmentally damaging?**

3 **How has Kenya managed the impacts of tourism?**

Sustainable development

- Sustainable development aims to help us develop now and in the future.

- People have put forward plans to help us develop sustainably.

- Poverty and current rates of environmental destruction are two of the threats to sustainable development.

A What is sustainable development?

1 key fact One of the most well-used definitions is development that 'meets the needs of the present without compromising the ability of future generations to meet their own needs'.

There are many different definitions of sustainable development. This definition was used in a report published by the Brundtland Commission in 1987.

2 At a basic level, sustainable development is about people being able to continue living well now, but in a way that allows future generations to enjoy a good standard of living as well.

3 Those who support the desire for sustainable development believe that natural and human environments have a carrying capacity. This means they have a limit to how much human activity they can support. For example, a town or city may only be able to ensure a good quality of life for a certain number residents. If the area becomes overpopulated, quality of life may be reduced for some residents.

B What may sustainable development involve?

1 key fact Sustainable development aims to support the environment, economy and society.

2 Sustainable development may involve:

- conserving natural environments

- ensuring that supplies of natural resources are not exhausted (see pages 120-1)

- reducing waste and the misuse of resources

- protecting fragile ecosystems

- protecting and preserving areas of high biodiversity (see pages 72–5)

- reducing the impacts of climate change (see pages 68–9)

- protecting the world's seas and oceans

- ensuring that settlements are safe, with good standards of housing and transport for all

- establishing sustainable cities (e.g. zero-carbon cities) (see pages 88–9 on sustainable cities)

- ensuring that there are safe and secure job opportunities for all

- ensuring that extreme poverty is eradicated (see pages 106–7)

- reaching a stable level of population growth (see pages 78–9 on managing population growth in LEDCs)

- developing sustainable businesses and industry, e.g. ecotourism (see page 113 on ecotourism).

C How can sustainable development be achieved?

1 **key fact** Many international, national and local organisations are working towards achieving sustainable development. These organisations include governments, charities and NGOs.

2 In 1992 the UN held a conference on the environment and development. It was in Rio de Janeiro, Brazil, and has since become known as the Rio Earth Summit.

- A document or declaration was signed at the conference which outlined 27 ways in which people could help promote sustainable development across the world.

- The Rio Earth Summit was followed in 2002 by the World Summit on Sustainable Development (sometimes called the Earth Summit 2002) which was held in Johannesburg, South Africa.

3 At a national and local level many governments and councils have signed agreements and plans for sustainable development. In many countries, including England, local councils have produced local plans called Local Agenda 21.

Local Agenda 21 involves local people and organisations working together to lessen their impact on the natural environment and taking action to protect it in the future.

4 Some people believe that not enough progress has been made towards sustainable development.

They argue that there are many threats to achieving sustainability. Such threats include extreme poverty, conflict and the way in which the global economy operates (many businesses operate to make a profit and are not always sensitive to environmental concerns). Current levels of environmental destruction could also threaten attempts to achieve sustainable development.

Wind turbine near Boulogne-sur-mer, France

>> practice questions

1 **Explain what is meant by sustainable development.**

2 **Describe what sustainable development may involve in:**
a) a city, b) the tourism industry.

3 **Why do some people believe that sustainable development is not being achieved in some places?**

Sustainable resource use

> 🔧 Natural resources can be classified as renewable and non-renewable.
>
> 🔧 Extracting and using natural resources has an impact on people and the environment.
>
> 🔧 Reducing waste can help people to use resources sustainably.

A Resources

1  **key fact** A resource is something is useful or valuable to people.

2 Resources can be natural and human:

- Natural resources come from the earth, e.g. rocks or minerals. The landscape itself is a resource. For example, attractive and interesting landscapes are important resources for the tourist industry.

- People provide human resources. For example, a steelworker in a steel factory has important skills that are a resource to the steel company.

3 Natural resources can be classified (organised) into two groups:

- **Non-renewable resources.** There are limited supplies of these resources and they cannot be replaced once they have been used. Non-renewable resources include coal, oil and natural gas.

- **Renewable resources.** These resources will not run out or they can be replaced. This means they can be used again and again. Renewable resources include wind, sun and water.

B Extracting natural resources

1 Many of the natural resources we use, for example, coal and oil, have to be extracted (taken) from within the Earth.

2 The process of extracting fossil fuels can have impacts upon people and the natural environment.

Case study – coal mining

- Coal mining involves extracting coal from within the Earth. In the past, coal mining involved removing coal from seams close to or at the Earth's surface. As technology has developed, it has become possible to mine deeper beneath the Earth's surface.
- Accessible supplies of coal in the UK, are now beginning to run out.
- The UK now imports some of its coal supplies from other countries, including LEDCs.

remember >>

Extracting raw materials is classified as a primary industry.

Creates employment and income for people and places.

Benefits of coal mining – mainly social or economic

Strong communities can develop in mining towns, for example in the Welsh Valleys.

Coal is used to generate power for factories and industry. Industries generate wealth and income for a country and its workers.

When a mine is opened, other services and industries are attracted to locate close by. This sets off the multiplier effect (see page 112).

Mining can be difficult and dangerous.

Problems created by coal mining – mainly environmental

Large amounts of land are destroyed for opencast mining. It is hard to re-landscape old mining areas.

Once a coalfield is exhausted and all the coal has been mined, it will close. This can have serious impacts on mining communities.

Coal mining produces waste rocks and materials. These materials are stored in piles called spoil tips. Spoil tips create unattractive landscapes.

Mining creates heavy traffic and noise pollution.

C Sustainable resource use

 The demand for natural resources is increasing at both a national and global level. Natural resources are used to generate power, manufacture products and produce food.

- MEDCs consume most of the world's resources. LEDCs tend to consume far less.

- It is estimated that if everyone in the world lived like we do in the UK, we would need two-and-a-half planet Earths to provide our needs.

- It is argued that our current use of natural resources is unsustainable. Supplies of some resources, such as coal, have begun to run out and the level of waste produced by homes and businesses is high.

 Reducing waste is a key priority for many local, national and international groups.

- The three R's are an important part of waste management: Reduce, Reuse and Recycle.

- Reducing our demand for resources and cutting the amount that we waste is seen as the most desirable option. Reusing and recycling waste help achieve this aim.

3 Money is also being invested in researching and developing sustainable alternatives to the resources we currently use.

4 As LEDCs begin to industrialise and develop, the global demand for resources will rise. More and more pressure will be placed upon limited supplies of natural resources.

>> practice questions

1 **Explain the difference between renewable and non-renewable energy sources.**

2 **Describe the impacts of coal mining upon people and the environment.**

3 **How can the way in which humans use resources be made more sustainable?**

Resources and energy production

 Most of the world's energy is generated by burning non-renewable fossil fuels.

 Sustainable energy production involves using renewable energy resources.

A Generating energy

Natural resources are used in large amounts to produce energy such as electricity or gas. This energy is used to power homes, transport and industry.

Non-renewable energy sources	Renewable energy sources
Coal, oil, natural gas, nuclear power (however, very small amounts of uranium are used to produce nuclear power, therefore some argue it is a sustainable energy source)	Hydro-electric power, wind power, tidal power, solar power, geothermal energy (using the Earth's natural heat), fuelwood (mainly used in LEDCs)

B Non-renewable energy sources

 key fact Oil, coal, natural gas are non-renewable fossil fuels.

- Most of the world's energy is generated by burning coal, oil and natural gas.

- Burning fossil fuels can have serious impacts on the environment. Global warming (see pages 66–7 on climate change) and acid rain are two major concerns.

 Acid rain is caused by air pollution from power stations and factories. Sunlight converts emissions of sulphur dioxide (SO_2 and nitrogen oxide (NO_2) into sulphuric acid and nitric acid. Moisture in the atmosphere dissolves these, turning them into weak acids. This acid falls to the Earth as rainfall.

- Acid rain can be carried large distances by the wind. Large areas of Scandinavia including Norway and Sweden have been affected by acid rain.

- Acid rain can pollute rivers and lakes; this pollution can kill fish. Acid rain can also damage trees and destroy forest areas.

- Many environmental groups and international organisations are trying to reduce the use of fossil fuels and minimise environmental damage.

	Advantages ✔	Disadvantages ✖
Coal	• Available in many countries • Large reserves remain relatively untouched	• Burning coal creates pollution and is linked to acid rain. • Releasing carbon dioxide is linked to the onset of global warming (see pages 66–7). • Mining can be dangerous and damages the environment.
Oil	• An efficient source of energy • A diverse energy source with many uses • Easily transported via pipelines, tankers and lorries.	• Air pollution is created • Releases carbon dioxide • Danger of oil spills in seas and oceans

	Advantages	Disadvantages
Natural gas	• An efficient source of energy. Little waste is produced • Cleaner than other fossil fuels • Easy to transport via pipelines	• Some air pollution is created • Releases carbon dioxide • Highly flammable (fires and explosions can be caused)

C Renewable energy sources

>> **key fact** In recent years many countries have begun to develop and use renewable energy sources.

Renewable energy sources tend to be clean and environmentally friendly; they produce little waste or pollution. Renewable energy sources are considered sustainable.

	Advantages ✓	Disadvantages
Wind power	• Wind turns blades on large turbines to generate electricity. • Wind power does not produce waste or pollution. • Relatively cheap to produce	• Wind turbines need to be placed on exposed, undeveloped landscapes. • Lots of turbines are needed to produce a useful amount of energy. • Many people feel that wind turbines are unattractive and noisy.
Solar power	• Solar panels or photovoltaic cells use sunlight to produce electricity. • Solar power does not produce waste or pollution. • It is relatively cheap and efficient.	• The technology needed to produce solar power is expensive to develop and install. • Solar energy cannot be generated at night or in very cloudy conditions.
Geothermal power	• Water is heated using the Earth's natural heat. This produces steam, which turns turbines. • There are lots of potential sites for geothermal energy (many are in LEDCs).	• Sulphuric gases are produced as a by-product of the geothermal energy. • It is expensive to develop geothermal energy and maintenance costs can be high.

D Nuclear energy

>> **key fact** As supplies of fossil fuels run low and environmental concerns grow, many countries have developed nuclear power.

Nuclear power is cleaner and more efficient than fossil fuels, and does not release greenhouse gases or create acid rain. However, many people are concerned about the safety of nuclear power, particularly after the accident at Chernobyl in the Ukraine, in 1986. The nuclear debate is a controversial one, with strong opinions and arguments on both sides.

>> practice questions

1 List two disadvantages of using fossil fuels to generate energy.

2 Explain why acid rain is an international problem.

3 Outline the costs and benefits of using wind power.

Managing water resources

- Worldwide water consumption is increasing.

- Water is mainly used in homes, industry and farming.

- In the UK most people live in areas with limited water supplies. The areas with good supplies of water are sparsely populated.

- Water supplies can be managed in a number of ways.

A Water sources and water use

1 **key fact** Water for our supply system comes from aquifers, reservoirs and rivers.

- Aquifers are large bodies of porous rock that can hold very large amounts of water.

- Reservoirs are artificial lakes created by building a dam across a valley and allowing it to flood.

2 **key fact** People in MEDCs consume about three times more water than people in LEDCs.

- Most water in LEDCs is used in farming, mainly for irrigation. In MEDCs, industry uses about 50% of the water available.

- Much less water is used in homes in LEDCs as far fewer people have piped water supplies.

3 The demand for water increases in LEDCs as industry and tourism develop. Rising living standards mean that people are using more water at home too. However, many LEDCs do not have the money or resources to manage their water supplies efficiently.

B Global water surplus and deficit

1 Places that receive more water from precipitation than they lose through evapotranspiration have a water surplus (e.g. Japan).

2 Places that lose more water from evapotranspiration than they receive from precipitation have a water deficit (e.g. Egypt).

- Many places have a balance between the two (e.g. France).

- As water consumption increases, many water sources are drying up from being used too much. When the demand for water exceeds the amount available, water stress occurs.

> **remember >>**
>
> **Many countries have built dams and reservoirs so that they can manage water supplies and control flooding at the same time.**

C Water supply issues

>> **key fact** The problems facing the demand for water differ between MEDCs and LEDCs.

- In MEDCs like the UK the main issues are:
  - maintaining good water quality
  - leaks
  - the imbalance between rainfall and population. The heaviest rainfall occurs in the north and west of the UK; however, most people live in the southeast, which is the driest part of the UK.

- In LEDCs like India the main issues are:
  - water pollution from industry (manufacturing and mining) and farming in particular
  - access to safe water
  - diseases (cholera, typhoid and bilharzias) from contaminated water.

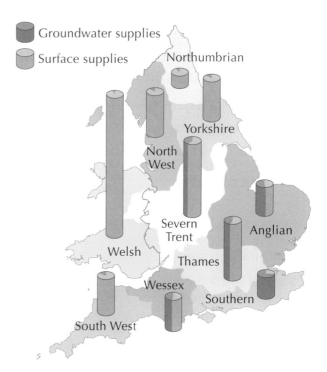

D Water management

 key fact **In MEDCs water is managed by water authorities.**

In the UK, water authorities have used a range of measures to try to manage water use and prevent water shortages:

- Advertising campaigns have been shown on television and radio to encourage people not to waste water by fitting dual-flush toilets or cistern displacement devices.

- Water authorities have installed water meters.

- During the summer months, some water authorities have imposed hosepipe bans in dry areas. This affects people who use water in their gardens and for cleaning their cars. It also affects public areas such as parks and golf courses.

key fact **In LEDCs most water management is carried out at a local level.**

This often involves using appropriate technology. For example, NGOs like Water Aid may train local people to operate rainwater harvesters or tube wells.

Large-scale water management projects are also used in LEDCs. This tends to involve constructing large dams, such as the Bargi Dam on the Narmarda River in India (this took 14 years to construct and cost around 100 million US dollars).

>> practice questions

1 **Using the diagram above, describe the pattern of water supply in England and Wales.**

2 **Make a list of possible water management techniques.**

3 **Explain why water management is often harder in LEDCs than MEDCs.**

Exam questions and model answers

This section provides two things:

1 General exam advice, including how to prepare for and how to tackle different kinds of questions and papers.

2 Some sample questions with answers and examiners' explanations, showing why these answers achieve full marks.

Important note

There are many different specifications for geography, offered by a range of exam boards. Each specification has different requirements and places different demands on students. This section aims to provide you with general guidance and advice to help you prepare for your exams. You should speak to your teacher for specific advice regarding the course you are following.

In September 2009 new GCSE courses began in England and Wales, therefore the style of the exam papers may evolve and change over time. The advice below has been based on sample exam papers provided by the various exam boards.

About geography GCSE exams

1 Tiered papers

For GCSE geography exams, you can be entered at different levels: Foundation Tier or Higher Tier. This is to give everyone the chance to get the best grade they can. Your teacher will have decided which is the best tier for you. If you are entered for Foundation Tier you can access grades C–G. If you are entered for Higher Tier you can access grades A*–D (if you are very close to a D grade you may be awarded an E grade).

Foundation Tier questions are presented in a very clear way. Common formats for some of the questions include multiple-choice, tick boxes and fill the gaps. You will have to write some longer answers, but the amount of space given in your answer booklet will give you a clear idea of how long your answers should be.

The questions on Higher Tier exams will be of a similar style to Foundation Tier but there will be fewer multiple-choice questions and you will be expected to complete more extended writing. Higher Tier exams also require you to make detailed use of examples and offer more reasons or explanations in your answers.

For both Foundation and Higher Tier papers it is likely that you will write the answers in a booklet. The questions will be printed in the booklet along with space to write the answers.

2 Dealing with pre-release materials

Some exam boards include an exam that involves you being sent materials to look at in advance. For these exams you tend to be given a booklet approximately 4–6 weeks before the exam. Inside the booklet there are several different resources, e.g. maps, photos, tables of data, graphs and charts. These resources will help you investigate a geographical issue selected from a part of your geography syllabus. The exam will test your skills at using these resources.

When you receive the booklet, your teacher may cover relevant ideas and topics to help you prepare for the exam. As well as preparing for this exam with your teacher, you should make your own notes. Look at what the resources in the booklet show, the key information presented and any geographical ideas and processes relevant to the issue. Make sure you understand the geographical terms used in the resources. If you have time, improve your background knowledge of the issue. Some students find it helpful to work in small study groups to discuss the issues the resources raise. Other students find web forums useful. Check carefully whether you will be sitting an exam that uses pre-release materials.

3 Decision-making skills

Some exam boards set exams that require candidates to make geographical decisions about an issue. Although the structure of questions varies between different exam boards, they all follow a similar sequence. Early questions ask you to interpret resources and outline the issues involved. You may then be asked to rank the solutions to the problem posed by the issue and/or evaluate solutions. You should be aware of the advantages and disadvantages of the solutions. Finally you are asked to decide which option/solution you would choose and justify your selection. You can develop your decision-making skills throughout your GCSE course by looking at and practising past papers or specimen papers. If there is a current geographical issue in your local area, decide what you think should be done about it.

4 Command words

Annotate	Add notes or comments to labels on maps or diagrams to explain what they show.
Compare	Identify and write down the similarities and differences between features or places stated in the question.
Complete	You might be asked to add the remaining parts of a diagram, map or graph.
Contrast	Write down and point out clearly the differences between the features or places.
Define	Write a definition of, meaning describe accurately or explain the meaning of.
Describe	Write down details about what is shown in a resource such as a map or diagram.
Discuss	Usually requires a longer answer, describing and giving reasons or explaining the arguments for and against.
Draw	You might be asked to draw a sketch map or diagram with labels to identify particular features.
Explain (or **Account for**)	Give reasons for the location or appearance of a particular feature.
Factors	Reasons for something such as the location of particular geographical features.
Give your views	You might be asked to say what you think or what another person or group might think.
Identify	Name, locate, recognise or select a particular feature or features (usually from a map, photograph or diagram).
List	Make a list of points. The number of marks tells you how many points to list (you may be given a numbered grid on which to write, particularly at Foundation level).
Locate	Write down where a feature or place is.
Mark	You may be asked to indicate or show where particular features are on a diagram or map.
Name, state or list	Write down accurate details or features.
Study	Look carefully at a resource and think about what it shows.
With reference to (or **refer to**) **examples that you have studied**	You need to include details about specific case studies or examples when explaining the reasons for a particular answer.
With the help of (or **using**) **the information provided**	Be sure to include examples from the information on the paper to explain your answer.

Answering exam questions about maps

In your geography exam you are very likely to be asked to use resources to help you answer specific questions. These resources tend to be presented in the form of a resource booklet. The types of resources found in the booklet may include: Ordnance Survey maps, sketches, photos, outline maps, tables and graphs.

When you are asked to refer to a resource to help you with a question in the exam paper, it is really important that you do so. Quote evidence directly from the resource. For example, if it is a map give grid references; if it is a graph quote figures.

If you are given a photograph to use it may be linked to a map, it may be on its own or it may be part of a selection of photographs. Make sure you describe what you can see in the photograph in as much detail as possible, using geographical words. You should also try to be as precise as possible.

Foundation

Use the map of the Keswick area on page 130 to answer the following questions:

>> Specimen question 1

What is the four-figure grid reference for the grid square containing Goosewell Fm?

A 2625

B 2923

C 2419

D 2525   1 mark

>> Model answer 1

2923

>> Specimen question 2

There is a peak called High Tove close to Keswick. In which grid square does the peak appear? Tick the correct box below:

2419 ☐

2816 ☐   1 mark

>> Model answer 2

2816

>> Specimen question 3

Circle the correct words from the options in the passage below:

Keswick is found **inland/on the coast**. It is a located next to a large **lake/beach**.

Tourists may visit the town because it has two museums and an **information**

centre/golf course. There is also a **lookout point/picnic site** to the south of the town.   3 marks

>> Model answer 3

Keswick is found inland/~~on the coast~~. It is a located next to a large lake/~~beach~~. Tourists may visit the town because it has two museums and an information centre/~~golf course~~. There is also a look out point/~~picnic site~~ to the south of the town.

Higher

>> Specimen question 1

What is the six-figure grid reference for the car park in Keswick?

_____   1 mark

>> Model answer 1

266229

>> Specimen question 2

Grid squares 2826 and 2817 are both areas of high land.
Which one has the steepest land?

_____   1 mark

>> Model answer 2

2826

>> Specimen question 3

Using the map, give three reasons why tourists may be attracted to this area.

_____

_____

_____ 3 marks

>> Model answer 3

Tourists may want to visit Keswick and the surrounding area because of the lake.
They may want to enjoy views of the lake or take part in water sports on the lake, e.g. sailing.
Tourists may also want to visit one of the two museums in the town of Keswick (found in square 2623).

This answer would be awarded all three marks. It gives three distinct reasons for visiting the area (enjoying the views, taking part in water sports and visiting museums). The candidate makes excellent use of the resource they have been given. They show this by quoting a grid reference from the map.

Ordnance Survey map of the Keswick area
See the sample questions on page 128

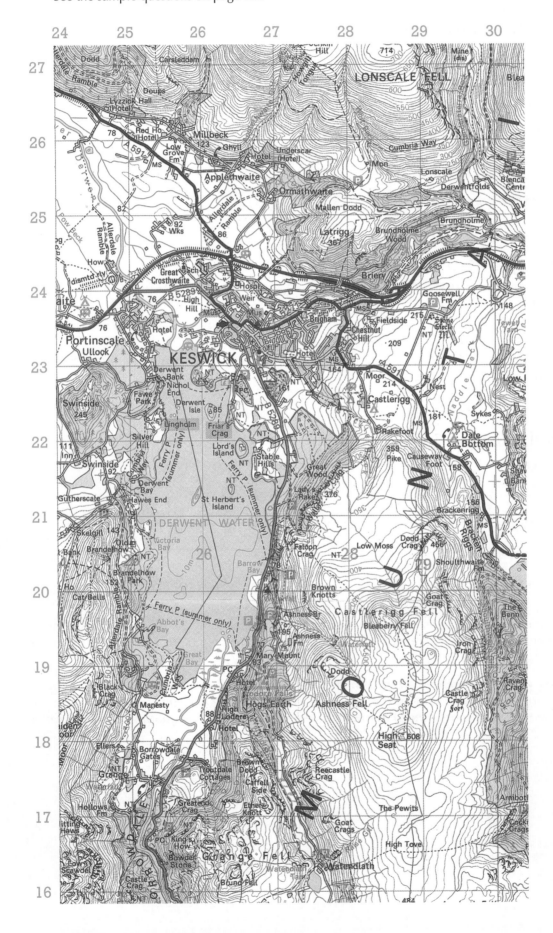

Key to Ordnance Survey symbols

ROADS AND PATHS
Not necessarily rights of way

Service area M 6   Elevated   Motorway (dual carriageway)
Junction number 41

Motorway under construction

Unfenced   Footbridge   Trunk road
A 6 (T)

Dual carriageway   Main road
A 592

Main road under construction

Secondary road
B 5305

Narrow road with passing places
A 855   B 885

Bridge   Road generally more than 4 m wide

Road generally less than 4 m wide

Other road, drive or track

Path

Gradient: 1 in 5 and steeper
1 in 7 to 1 in 5

Gates   Road tunnel

Ferry P   Ferry V   Ferry (passenger)   Ferry (vehicle)

PUBLIC RIGHTS OF WAY
(Not applicable to Scotland)

.... Footpath

---------- Bridleway

-·-·-·-·- Road used as a public path

-+-+-+-+- Byway open to all traffic

ANTIQUITIES

VILLA   Roman   ⚔ Battlefield (with date)   + Position of antiquity which cannot be drawn to scale
Castle   Non-Roman   ☆ Tumulus

𝔪 Ancient Monuments and Historic Buildings in the care of the Secretaries of State for the Environment, for Scotland and for Wales and that are open to the public

The revision date of archaeological information varies over the sheet

RAILWAYS

Track multiple or single   Freight line, siding or tramway
Track narrow gauge   Station (a) principal (b) closed to passengers
Bridges, Footbridge   Level crossing   LC
Tunnel   Embankment
Viaduct   Cutting

WATER FEATURES

Marsh or salting   Slopes   Cliff   High water mark
Towpath   Lock   Flat rock   Low water mark
Aqueduct   Canal   Ford   Lighthouse (in use)
Weir   Normal tidal limit   Sand   Beacon
Lake   Bridge   Dunes   Lighthouse (disused)
Footbridge   Mud   Shingle
Canal (dry)

TOURIST INFORMATION

🛈 🛈 Information centre, all year / seasonal
➳ Viewpoint
P Parking
✕ Picnic site
⚕ Camp site
🚐 Caravan site

▲ Youth hostel
▨ Selected places of tourist interest
📞 📞 Telephone, public/motoring organisation
⚑ Golf course or links
☐ PC Public convenience (in rural areas)

ABBREVIATIONS

P	Post office	CH	Clubhouse
PH	Public house	PC	Public convenience (in rural areas)
MS	Milestone	TH	Town Hall, Guildhall or equivalent
MP	Milepost	CG	Coastguard

GENERAL FEATURES

Electricity transmission line (with pylons spaced conventionally)
Pipe line (arrow indicates direction of flow)
ruin   Buildings
Public buildings (selected)
Bus or coach station
Coniferous wood
Non-coniferous wood
Mixed wood
Orchard
Park or ornamental grounds
Quarry
Spoil heap, refuse tip or dump
Radio or TV mast
Places of Worship — with tower / with spire, minaret or dome / without such additions
Chimney or tower
Glasshouse
Graticule intersection at 5' intervals
Ⓗ Heliport
△ Triangulation pillar
Windmill with or without sails
Windpump/wind generator

HEIGHTS

—— 50 —— Contours are at 10 metres vertical interval
·144 Heights are to the nearest metre above mean sea level

ROCK FEATURES

outcrop   cliff   scree

Heights shown close to a triangulation pillar refer to the station height at ground level and not necessarily to the summit.

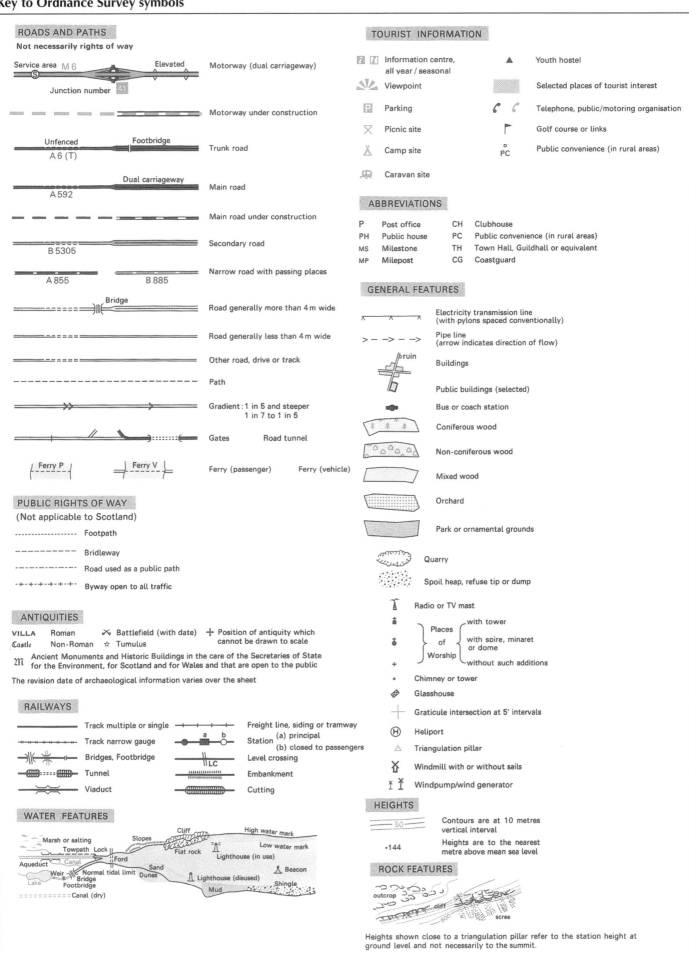

131

Foundation

>> Specimen question 1

Give two reasons why it is important to conserve areas of tropical rainforest.

1 _____

_____

2 _____

_____ **2 marks**

>> Model answer 1

1 People may want to conserve rainforest areas so that they can protect the habitats of rare animals.

2 People may also want to protect traditional tribes living in the forest.

>> Specimen question 2

In the future many countries are likely to be affected by global warming.
For one country you have studied, explain how global warming may affect the area in the future.

Name of country studied: _____

_____

_____

_____

_____

_____

_____

_____

_____

_____ **6 marks**

>> Model answer 2

Name of country studied: Bangladesh

Bangladesh is a very flat country. It is close to sea level. This means that it could be affected by rising sea levels if global warming happens. This could mean that parts of the country flood. People may lose their homes and people could be killed. Bangladesh is an LEDC and so it would find it hard to cope with this problem. Global warming could also affect farming in Bangladesh. Farmers may find it hard to grow their usual crops because the weather and climate have changed. Bangladesh suffers from cyclones. If global warming happens this could mean more cyclones. This could destroy people's houses and could kill people.

This answer would be awarded the full six marks as it makes three clear points about the effects of global warming (flooding, changing farming patterns and more extreme weather). The candidate then explains each point. This gains them the top marks. Note the candidate states that global warming may happen; remember it is not certain (some people argue it is not happening).

Higher

>> Specimen question 1

Explain why it is important to conserve areas of tropical rainforest.

_____
_____
_____
_____
_____
_____
_____
_____
_____ **4 marks**

>> Model answer 1

People may want to conserve areas of tropical rainforests because they are important ecosystems which are home to many rare plants and animals. The forest is the habitat for these animals. People may also want to protect the traditional tribes that live in the forest. Rainforest tribes live in harmony with the forest and know how to use the plants and animals sustainably. Their way of life can be destroyed if people try to develop the forest.

This answer would be awarded the full four marks as it makes two clear points about conserving the forest (protecting the plants and animals that live there and helping protect rainforest tribes) and then explains each one in detail using connectives (e.g. they explain that the forest is an important habitat for the animals that live there). The answer is very well structured. Note how they have used the word 'sustainable' (see pages 118–19).

>> Specimen question 2

In the future many countries are likely to be affected by global warming.
For one country you have studied, explain how global warming may affect people and the economy in the future.

_____
_____
_____
_____
_____
_____
_____
_____
_____
_____
_____ **6 marks**

>> Model answer 2

I have studied Bangladesh, which is an LEDC located in Asia. It is a very low-lying country and a lot of areas are close to sea level. If global warming is happening, sea levels may rise (due to melting ice caps). This could mean that parts of the country would suffer from flooding. Flooding would affect people badly. It could destroy buildings and some people might even lose their homes. Global warming could also affect farming in Bangladesh. Higher temperatures could mean that farmers can't grow the crops that they usually do. At the moment Bangladesh suffers from cyclones. If global warming happens they could have more extreme weather and more cyclones. This could destroy people's houses and could kill people. Bangladesh is an LEDC and so it would find it hard to cope with these problems.

This answer would be awarded the full six marks as it makes three clear points about the effects of global warming (increased flooding, changing farming patterns and more cases of extreme weather). The candidate explains each of their points using connectives (e.g. they explain that sea levels may rise because of melting ice caps). The answer is well structured. Note the candidate states that global warming may be happening; remember it is not certain (some people argue it is not happening).

Answers to practice questions

Using maps 1

1 0720

2 075203

Using maps 2

1 Tatton Farm

2 **a)** public telephone
   b) church with a tower
   c) golf course

3 50 metres above sea level

Using images and analysing data

1 Possible land uses include: leisure and tourism, transport, accommodation and catering (restaurants).

2 Answer must refer to evidence from the photograph. May include: warm temperatures (clear blue sky and good weather are shown in the photograph), plenty of accommodation, there is access to a large beach and also the sea. The sea can be used for water sports and swimming.

3 Answer must refer to evidence from the photograph and should address the effects on people and the cnvironment. Try to give a balance of positive and negative. Effects on the environment may include: busy, congested beaches which could lead to litter being left on the beach; possible water pollution from water sports; dense collection of high-rise buildings means a loss of open space. However, some special environments in the area may be protected, as tourists like to visit them.
Effects on people may include: local people perhaps not liking the high-rise buildings; the government may have introduced laws to limit the height of buildings; local people may find the tourists noisy. However, locals will be able to find work in the hotels and restaurants shown in the image.

Using new technologies in geography

1 There is a band of cloud going from north to south through Europe covering Sweden, parts of Germany, Poland, southern France and northeast Spain. There is also cloud cover in the Atlantic off the coast of Ireland and Cornwall.

2 GIS may help many different groups of people and industries. It can be used to help: the police (to record and track crimes, identify patterns and try to prevent crime), town planners and the local council (to map out urban areas in detail and plan out changes e.g. new housing or facilities) and the travel industry (to map out tourist facilities including hotels, transport links and attractions).

Tectonic hazards 1

1 The Indo-Australian plate

2 Most of the world's major earthquake and volcano zones are found on or near plate boundaries.

3 The South American plate and African plate or the North American plate and Eurasian plate

Tectonic hazards 2

1 A destructive plate boundary can be found where the Pacific and Eurasian plates meet. Another destructive boundary is found where the Nazca plate meets the South American plate.

2 Your answer should include the following information:

Two plates meet and denser oceanic crust is forced underneath continental crust. Oceanic plate sinks and melts in the subduction zone to form magma. Magma rises up through cracks in the rock to form volcanoes. The friction created as the plates move may cause earthquakes.

3 Folding occurs when continental crust is pushed upwards to form fold mountains.

Earthquakes

1 **a)** Focus: the point below the Earth's surface where pressure is released causing an earthquake
   b) Epicentre: the point on the Earth's surface directly above the focus

2 Your answer should explain that LEDCs tend to have less money and fewer resources to try and reduce the impacts of an earthquake, e.g. earthquake-proof buildings. They also have limited money to help rebuild an area and/or rehouse people after an earthquake. Also, with less money and fewer resources, it is difficult for the emergency services to cope with disasters such as earthquakes.

3 Your answer should include: The name of the example; the key facts about the earthquake (date and strength); key facts about the social impacts of the earthquake (lives lost, damage to buildings and roads); effects on the economy (cost of repair and rebuilding).

Volcanoes

1 Volcanoes form when magma escapes from within the mantle. The magma forces its way through weaknesses in the Earth's crust. As the magma rises, a build-up of pressure occurs and this causes a volcanic explosion. When the magma reaches the Earth's surface, it becomes lava and cools to form new rock. After many explosions, this rock builds up to form a volcanic mountain. The process of folding (see page 12) can also form volcanoes.

2 Your answer should include: the name of a volcanic zone (e.g. areas of Japan, the Philippines or Iceland), an explanation of the different advantages that a volcano can bring people:
– adding rich nutrients to the soil, which helps agriculture
– income from tourism helps the economy
– health benefits from hot volcanic springs
– not wanting to leave the area or not having a choice about leaving.
You must explain why each point is important and develop your ideas.

Case study: Sichuan earthquake

1 15 million people were displaced, nearly 70 000 died and 375 000 injured. 5 million homes were lost. There were many landslides creating quake lakes in upland areas. Around 12 million animals were killed. Liquid ammonia leaked from two factories which had collapsed (damaging the environment).

2 It lies at the boundary of two plates, (Indo-Australian and Eurasian). The province is densely populated and quality controls on building are not very tight.

Mt Nyiragongo volcano

1 Two parts of the African plate were pulled apart along a fault line.

2 In the short term a Red Alert was issued, the UN sent aid, Oxfam set up camps and the WHO gave vaccinations. In the long term the UN spent a year resettling the homeless and helping people back to work.

3 Most people have strong tribal links to the area and are either farmers or fishermen. They rely on the lake and the soils of Mt Nyiragongo to make a living.

Tropical storms

1 They develop over large bodies of warm water in the tropics. The sea temperature causes moist air to rise releasing large amounts of heat resulting in condensation of water vapour and formation of huge storm clouds.

2 A large, low pressure system, with thunderstorms that produce strong winds and heavy rain.

3 People should have a family plan and a disaster kit, secure their homes and go to a cyclone shelter nearby. Planting mangrove swamps and building cyclone walls can also limit the damage.

Drought

1 When there is not enough precipitation to support life

2 By overusing water and cutting down too many trees

3 Sub-tropical high pressure sits over the Sahel preventing wet air at the equator from moving in.

4 They have to move southwards to savannah in neighbouring countries, or away from the countryside altogether to start a new life in the city.

Rocks and weathering

1 Weathering involves the break up of rocks on the Earth's surface. Erosion involves the wearing away of the Earth's surface.

2 Igneous rock is formed when magma reaches the Earth's surface and cools to form new rock.

3 Weak acids in rainwater easily dissolve limestone. When a stream or river flows over limestone it dissolves joints in the rock and then disappears down into the rock and flows underground until it reaches an area of impermeable rock. This process of chemical weathering helps to form underground caves.

Glaciation

1 Your answer should explain the processes of abrasion and plucking.

2 In your answer you should name a glaciated environment, e.g. the Lake District. You should then explain that glaciated landscapes are made up of very distinctive landforms and features. This makes them attractive to tourists and day visitors. Glaciated landscapes are also ideal for outdoor activities, e.g. hill walking, climbing and abseiling. However, many glaciated landscapes are National Parks and are protected environments. This can cause conflict between those who want to visit and use the landscape and those who want to protect it.

The river system

1 **a)** A drainage basin is the area of land drained by a river and its tributaries.

b) A watershed is the boundary between two drainage basins, usually found on a highland region.

c) A tributary is a small stream or river which joins the main river channel.

d) A confluence is the point where two rivers meet.

2 Some water may fall directly into a river channel as precipitation, water may also reach the river by moving through the soil (throughflow) or by moving through the rock layer (groundwater flow). Some water may also travel overland towards a river (surface runoff).

3 Water can be stored as ice in a glacier, on the surface as a lake or below ground in the rock or soil layer.

River processes

1 Abrasion: small pebbles and rocks that are transported by the river wear away the riverbed.
Attrition: pebbles and rocks being transported by the river knock together and break down into smaller particles.
Hydraulic action: the force of the water wears away the river bed and banks.
Solution: weak acids in the water dissolve the rocks.

2 A river may transport natural material by traction, saltation, suspension or solution. An explanation should be given of each term.

River landscapes and features

1 List may include: waterfalls, gorges, rapids and V shaped valleys.

2 Diagram should include labels to show areas of erosion and deposition, the neck of the meander, the direction of flow and the line of the fastest flow within the river.

3 Your answer should include a named example, e.g. the Ganges Delta, and some brief locational information. Explain the advantages of living around the lower course of a river, e.g. flat land (good for farming, industry and construction), good access and potential for trade with other countries (ports) and rich fertile farmland.

Flooding and hydrographs

1 Humans can increase the risk of flooding by building on the floodplain (concrete is impermeable and vegetation that could intercept the rainwater is lost) and engineering the river channel (making it deeper or wider).

2 Peak discharge was reached after 16 hours.

3 Graph A shows river discharge for an urban area. Evidence for this includes the short lag time (5 hours) and the steep rising limb. This shows that water has reached the river channel quickly, which suggests that the area around the river is built up and urbanised, with little vegetation. It could also be surrounded by highland.

Managing flooding

1 Your answer should include a discussion of hard engineering options (e.g. building a dam or modifying the river channel) and a discussion of soft engineering options (e.g. afforestation and changing planning regulations). Try and name rivers where some of these methods have been tried.

2 Your answer should include:
– the name of the river studied and a description of its location
– a brief explanation of the methods that have been used to help control flooding along the river (e.g. building a dam).
You should explain:
– the advantages of what has been done to the river for people (e.g. saving lives, generating hydroelectric power)
– the advantages of what has been done to the river for the environment (e.g. planting trees around the river)
– the disadvantages of what has been done to the river for people (e.g. losing homes to build the dam)
– the disadvantages of what has been done to the river for the environment (e.g. preventing the natural flooding of the river).

Wave power

1 Waves are created when wind blows over the sea's surface. Friction from the sea bed helps form the waves.

2 A wave's energy is controlled by its strength, duration and fetch.

3 Fetch is the distance a wave travels.

4 Constructive waves are longer, flatter, gentler and have a strong swash. They build beaches. Destructive waves are taller, shorter in length and have strong backwash. They erode beaches.

Coastal processes

1 Waves break at an angle to the beach (due to the prevailing wind). At X the swash of the wave pushes material up the beach at an angle. Material is moved back down towards the sea (by gravity and by the backwash). This happens at a right angle. Waves continue to push material along the beach in this way until it reaches Y. This is called longshore drift.

2 When waves lose energy.

3 Less resistant rocks, such as clay, erode easily and quickly. Resistant rocks, such as granite, erode more slowly.

4 The rock type will determine the extent to which different types of weathering are possible (e.g. limestone cliffs will be easily affected by chemical weathering). The rock types found in a cliff will also influence the chances of a landslide. Weaker rocks will be more easily attacked by waves and weathering and therefore a landslide may be more possible.

Landforms created by erosion

1 A 'notch' is formed at the base of a cliff.

2 Hard rocks such as chalk are associated with headlands.

3 A = cave
B = arch
C = stack
D = wave-cut platform

Depositional landforms

1 Beaches are made through the transportation and then deposition of material by the sea. Constructive waves build beaches.

2

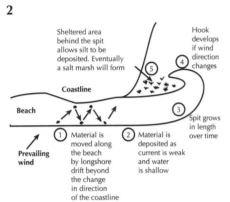

3 See sketch above

4 The area behind the spit is sheltered and the sea is calm. This makes it attractive and safe for swimming. The spit provides long stretches of sandy beaches and interesting habitats e.g. mud flats or salt marshes. People may go bird watching in such areas.

Managing the coastline

1 The government (Environment Agency) and local councils

2 Hard management strategies are usually more expensive than soft management strategies. They are usually visually intrusive and less sustainable. Soft engineering is less costly and often more sustainable.

3 Groynes: these prevent the movement of beach material along the coast allowing the beach to build up as a defence against erosion and to act as an attraction for tourists. However they do not last long as the wood rots and can look ugly.

Rip rap: these look quite natural and absorb wave energy thus protecting the land and buildings behind from erosion. However they can be expensive and will still let some waves through.

Coastal case studies

1 Erosion is a problem in Happisburgh due to the geology of the cliffs (they are made up of soft clay and sand). They are not very resistant to erosion. The waves attacking the cliffs are made powerful by the long fetch (they are particularly destructive during winter storms). As well as being eroded by the sea, weathering also takes place along the face and top of the cliff (this can lead to mass movements).

2 Happisburgh has some defences (groynes and revetments), however many of these are broken. The government has decided not to protect Happisburgh from erosion in the future. Local people have signed petitions and campaigned for more action to protect their village. Some rock armour was added to the beach in 2007.

3 Farmland behind the shingle ridge has been abandoned and the freshwater marsh is changing to saltwater, altering rare natural habitats.

4 Moving people and activities back from the affected areas and allowing natural processes to happen is sustainable because the land does not have great economic value, relatively few people live there and climate change is likely to cause significant sea level rise in the area anyway.

5 Local tourist businesses, farmers and residents because they will lose their livelihoods and homes.

Weather and climate

1 Weather: condition of the atmosphere on a particular day
Climate: average or expected condidions for a specific place, for a certain time of the year

2 a) Berlin: 19 °C, Rome: 23 °C. They differ because Berlin has a central European (transition) climate and Rome has a Mediterranean climate.

b) Berlin has a greater temperature range because it is a continental climate, whereas Shannon has a maritime climate.

c) Shannon has the highest annual precipitation.

UK weather

1 Polar Maritime and Tropical Maritime

2 Polar Maritime, Arctic Maritime and Polar Continental

3 Tropical Maritime and Tropical Continental

4 Much of the UK's rainfall is due to relief. Rain falls over the hills in the west. As air moves west to east it warms up. Therefore, the south and east of England are in the rain shadow and receive little rain.

Depressions and anticyclones

1 A is fine

2 B is cloudy

3 From the south-west

4 Thick cloud is associated with occluded fronts over the North Atlantic and the North Sea. These are caused by a large amount of warm moist air rising at these fronts, where a warm sector has been undercut by cold air moving in from a cold sector. A band of cloud is associated with the warm front over France. Warm air is rising over cool air. The cloud along the front is due to colder air undercutting warm air. This forces it to rise and cool, leading to condensation. Whirls of cloud associated with low pressure over the North Atlantic. Clear skies over Spain due to high pressure and no fronts over the Mediterranean.

Cold environments 2

1 In the Arctic and Antarctic Circles, N Canada and Alaska, N Russia and Scandinavia, Iceland

2 Long, cold winters below freezing and short summers. It is windy and quite dry all year round.

3 The harsh environment means there is only a short growing season for plants as few can thrive in permafrost. Only mammals can live here all year round as they have adapted to the cold conditions. Insects thrive in the short summer and birds also visit.

4 Prudhoe Bay: 1 million barrels of oil are extracted each day. The leaks from the pipelines have damaged the tundra and disrupted the migratory patterns of animals.

Antarctica: tourist ships dump grey waste and have introduced alien species here. Raft landings have a high impact when they happen on the same spaces of the Antarctic Peninsula time and time again.

5 It was the last major land mass to be explored and does not belong to any one country. All the signatories to the Antarctic Treaty recognise that it must be preserved for science and as a wilderness and so will not allow it to be exploited.

Hot desert environments 2

1 The Sahara is a trade wind desert. The Namib is a coastal desert. The Thar is a monsoon desert. The Arabian is a rain shadow desert.

2 Uluru: 400 000 people a year go there. Visitor trampling degrades the vegetation. Excessive numbers overuse scarce resources like water and create more pollution.

Gharwar: the bedrock is weakened by deep drill holes, flares emit greenhouse gases and pipelines disturb and destroy biota.

3 Nomads move from oasis to oasis. This movement of people and animals gives the land time to recover between visits. Reducing stock density has a similar effect as it relieves the pressure on the land. Planting trees helps to keep the soil in place as well as build up over time. This in turn increases the fertility and productivity of the land.

Climate change

1 The greenhouse effect is a natural process in which the heat from the sun is trapped in the atmosphere by greenhouse gases such as methane and carbon dioxide. It is argued that people are altering the greenhouse effect causing global warming.

2 Factories and power stations release CO_2, deforestation reduces the ability of forests to convert CO_2 into oxygen and methane is released through farming.

3 Throughout history there have been changes in temperature (cycles of warming and cooling). Some people believe that current patterns of global warming are part of a natural cycle of climate change.

Managing the impacts of climate change

1 List may include: sea level rise, flooding, glacial retreat, coral bleaching and unusual changes in our climate.

2 Measures may include: afforestation (planting trees), using more sustainable sources of energy, reducing energy use, local initiatives and international agreements.

3 Not everyone agrees that climate change is happening. This makes discussion about it controversial. It is also hard for everyone to agree on what should be done. Many LEDCs do not agree that they should reduce their carbon dioxide emissions as it will hold back their chances for development. Not all countries have signed up to current agreements or targets.

Ecosystems

1 Any three from the key on the map, e.g. tropical rainforest ecosystems, coniferous forest ecosystems and deciduous forest ecosystems.

2 In the desert there is very little fertile soil (mainly sand) and there is little or no rainfall. This lack of inputs into the system means that the desert cannot support a lot of plants or animals.

3 Name an ecosystem and explain how energy flows through the ecosystem in the form of a food chain. Name the species of plants and animals found in the food chain.

The rainforest ecosystem 2

1 Found mainly along the equator, between the tropics of Cancer and Capricorn

2 The reason for the rich diversity of plants and animals in the rainforest is the high number of inputs into the system, e.g. sunlight and rainfall.

3 Your example should include the name of the ecosystem and some brief locational information. Explain why humans have changed the ecosystem and what impacts this change has had on the ecosystem. For example, humans have changed the tropical rainforest ecosystem because it is an important resource (providing wood, minerals and land). People have cleared the trees (deforestation) to use these resources. This deforestation has had many impacts on the forest ecosystem (loss of animal and plant species, loss of oxygen, and a loss of nutrients in the soil).

Population change

1 The difference between the birth rate and the death rate.

2 At the start of the model birth rates and death rates are high, whilst the total population is low. As a country moves through the model the total population increases. This is because as a country develops, birth rates remain high for a while, whilst death rates fall (due to improved medical care). This leads to a period of high natural increase and rapid population growth. After time, birth rates also fall. In stage 4 and 5 a country has a low birth rate and a low death rate, but a high total population.

3 Tanzania has many young dependants (due to high birth rates) and few elderly dependants (due to low life expectancy). Japan has many elderly dependants (due to high life expectancy) and a declining number of young dependants (due to a falling birth rate).

Managing population change

1 Due to a high rate of natural increase (high birth rates and falling death rates).

2 Your answer should include: a named country or place that has tried to control population growth; this place may have tried to reduce or increase the birth rate. Describe what the country has done to control population growth and explain how these ideas or strategies changed the birth rate. For example, Derada, a Tanzanian village reduced its birth rate. A health centre was built in the village so that children could be vaccinated against disease and women could receive advice about family planning. This reduced infant mortality in the village and women could choose to have fewer children.

3 An ageing population is caused by an increase in the number of elderly people in a population (due to rising life expectancy) and a fall in the number of young people (due to declining birth rates).

4 To deal with an ageing population Japan is trying to raise the birth rate (e.g. the 'new angel policy'), reforming the pension system, allowing people to work beyond retirement and improving care for the elderly.

Migration

1 Net migration is the total number of immigrants minus the number of emigrants.

2 Push factors encourage people to leave an area. Push factors include: poor housing, unemployment, war, famine and crime.

3 Your answer should include the name of the source country and the host country (where have people migrated from [source country] and where have they gone to [host country]?). Discuss the positive impacts of migration on the source country (e.g. cheap labour) and on the host country (e.g. money may be sent home to family). You must also discuss the negative impacts of migration on the source country (e.g. loss of skilled workers) and the host country (e.g. possible tension and conflict if people fear that their jobs are being taken by migrants).

Urban settlement

1 Rates of urbanisation are low in MEDCs (as many people are moving to the edge of towns or cities and into rural areas). Rates of urbanisation are high in LEDCs (due to rural–urban migration and high rates of natural increase in cities).

2 Most MEDC cities have grown outwards from the centre. In the centre, land values are high and so buildings are built skywards. In the centre of the city (the CBD) the land is used for business, trade and administration. Around the CBD is the former industrial zone of the city. In many cities this area is now in decline and is a zone undergoing change. Around the edge of the former industrial zone is the poorest quality housing built during industrialisation for the workers. However, in some parts of this zone, gentrification has taken place and the housing has been improved. As you move out of the city, the quality of the housing improves. The suburbs on the edge of the city have lower density housing and larger homes with gardens.

3 In LEDCs the pattern of land use is different to MEDCs. Although LEDCs also have a CBD in the centre of the city, the lowest quality housing is found on the edge of the city. These are squatter settlements. High-quality homes can be found further inside the city or along the main routes out of the city.

Challenges facing MEDC cities

1 Your answer may include the following problems: inequalities in housing provision, access to services, quality of life and environmental quality.

2 Your answer should include: information about the history of the inner-city area (built during the Industrial Revolution to house factory workers), information about the decline of industry in the inner city and the problems that this then caused for the areas, i.e. the spiral of decline (loss of jobs, houses falling into disrepair, out migration and the closure of services).

3 The inner city can be regenerated or redeveloped. Redevelopment involves improving the physical environment of the area (clearing derelict buildings and refurbishing houses and flats), whilst regeneration tries to improve the area's economy and quality of life for the people living in that area (by creating jobs and improving services).

Challenges facing LEDC cities

1 Rural–urban migration and high natural increase in urban areas

2 People live in high densities in squatter settlements, they tend to have few amenities, e.g. running water, the waste disposal system may be poor and this can lead to disease. The squatter settlements tend to be far from the centre of the city where the jobs can be found.

3 Quality of life in squatter settlements may be improved by working with the residents of the area. Charities and governments may be involved in helping individuals and families. Some cities have introduced site-and-service schemes (people buy a piece of land connected to the main services of the city and build their own home). Self-help schemes can also be introduced whereby people are encouraged to improve their homes and gain ownership of the land.

Sustainable urban living

1 A sustainable city helps support society (everyone has access to suitable housing and services), the economy (good, long-term employment opportunities are available and resources are used sustainably) and the environment (threats to the environment are minimised; waste and pollution are reduced).

2 Traffic congestion can be reduced using park and ride schemes, traffic calming, congestion charging and good cycle networks.

3 Your answer should include the name of the urban area that you have studied and where it is. You should then describe what has been done to make it more sustainable and comment on how successful these measures have been.

Urban sprawl

1 Green belts were introduced to prevent urban sprawl (the outward growth of a town or city into the countryside).

2 The movement of people from urban areas to rural areas

3 Village services are declining as newcomers continue to shop in nearby towns where they work. Most will use their cars to get there. If they do not use existing bus services and shops in their village these will close down. This creates problems for some existing residents who cannot drive or do not have cars. The population structure of many villages is changing. In many coastal villages the population has become mostly elderly. This puts pressure on local health, housing and social services when these people become infirm.

Changing farming in MEDCs

1 Diversification involves using land for non-farming purposes.

2 Farmers can diversify in many ways including: opening a campsite, renting out farm cottages as holiday homes, setting up a bed and breakfast, selling farm produce and setting up craft centres.

3 Today, farmers are trying to reduce their environmental impact by restoring hedgerows, creating wildlife corridors and using EU grants to implement environmental schemes. Some farmers farm the land organically.

Changing farming in LEDCs

1 Most farming is subsistence, but can be either intensive or extensive. Some is nomadic. There is some commercial farming mainly on ranches and plantations.

2 To meet the needs of a growing population

3 By trying to reduce poverty and using local skills and appropriate technology to improve the quality of life for people. Also they are trying to farm sustainably and improve education and health care.

Globalisation

1 Modern transport technology means that we can visit places all over the world relatively quickly and easily. Communications technology, such as mobile phones and the internet, mean that we can communicate easily with people from other parts of the world. These developments have helped to create new connections between people and places. The world seems 'smaller'.

2 Positive impacts of globalisation include: people can travel around the world and communicate with people easily. Products from around the world are traded in most countries. Negative impacts of globalisation include: loss of traditional cultures and an unfair system of world trade. Also not everyone is experiencing globalisation.

3 TNCs are an important part of the global economy. They make a product in one country (or sometimes several countries) and export it around the world. This creates networks of travel and trade which contributes to globalisation.

The global economy

1 Possible answers include:

Primary	Secondary	Tertiary
farmer	builder	doctor
fishing	factory	train
miner	worker	driver
		teacher

2 X = 70% Primary, 10% Secondary 20% Tertiary

Y = 25% Primary, 45% Secondary 30% Tertiary

Z = 5% Primary, 25% Secondary 70% Tertiary

3 Transport costs, accessibility, land availability, labour supply, availability of raw materials etc.

Changing industry in MEDCs

1 The movement of manufacturing to somewhere else (mainly from MEDCs to LEDCs). This has happened because it is cheaper to manufacture goods in LEDCs. Supplies of raw materials running low (e.g. coal) is another cause of de-industrialisation.

2 Footloose industries are free to locate where they want to. They are not over-dependant on any single location factor.

3 It has declined due to the growth of MNCs and globalisation. As the UK's raw materials have depleted, other countries have developed competitive industries selling cheaper products. This is because in the UK raw materials and labour costs are high. Goods can now be produced more cheaply outside the UK.

Changing industry in LEDCs

1 It can be hard for an LEDC to industrialise because its people may be unskilled, the infrastructure underdeveloped and there may be little capital to make investments. Also current trading pattern favour MEDCs.

2 NIC stands for newly industrialising country. It is an LEDC that has been industrialised since the 1950s. NICs have industrialised rapidly.

3 NICs will place restrictions on imports of similar products to the ones they are producing to grow their own domestic markets. They may also devalue their own currency to make their products cheaper abroad and therefore more attractive to consumers overseas.

4 Benefits of industrialisation include increased living standards for workers.
Costs include the decimation of rural communities as the young move to the city to work in factories, and the dominance of western culture at the expense of traditional values.

Measuring global differences in development

1 Development can be measured using economic indicators such as GNP or HDI and social indicators such as life expectancy or literacy rates.

2 The MDGs aim to reduce poverty and inequality by setting targets to help eradicate world poverty by 2015. There are eight goals and over 180 countries have agreed to try to meet these. The goals include ending hunger, improving child health and combating HIV/Aids.

Trade, aid and development

1 LEDCs tend to spend more on importing manufactured goods than they make selling primary goods – this leads to a poor balance of trade.

2 LEDCs are often dependant on MEDCs for trade and aid due to their colonial past. Trade systems were set up many years ago when many LEDCs were colonies ruled by MEDCs. These trade systems benefited MEDCs. Even though colonisation ended during the last century, many LEDCs still rely on selling their primary products to MEDCs and buying manufactured goods from them.

3 Fair trade can ensure workers are paid a fair price for their products and are treated fairly. It can stop exploitation.

Tourism

1 People have more disposable income and paid holidays and more time to spend on a holiday. In addition, expectations and attitudes have changed and people expect to go on holiday at least once a year. Transport developments have also been very important, particularly the development of air travel.

2 Tourism can be classified according to the resources it uses (primary or secondary) or by location, activity, duration and distance travelled.

3 Your answer should include both positive and negative impacts on the environment, society and the economy:

Environment:
+ tourism income can help preserve areas
– tourism can harm fragile ecosystems

Society:
+ tourism can preserve local cultures (e.g. tourists pay to see traditional dances etc)
– there can be conflict between tourists and locals

Economy:
+ tourism creates jobs
– money can leak back to MEDCs.

Rural tourism in the UK

1 UK tourism was facing stiff competition from the Mediterranean and traditional seaside resorts were in decline.

2 A National Park is an area of relatively unspoilt scenic countryside that is protected against development.

3 Possible conflicts: disagreements between local residents, farmers and tourists. These disagreements may be caused due to the traffic congestion tourists create or tourists walking on farmland. The sheer number of tourists can put pressure on rural areas and cause conflicts.

4 The Yorkshire Dales National Park is being managed by improving public transport links to the parks (to reduce congestion), screening car parks with trees and restricting developments in honeypot areas.

Tourism issues in LEDCs

1 They are attractive because of hot year-round climates, beautiful scenery, different cultures and they're cheap.

2 The multiplier effect refers to the positive spin-offs resulting from a tourist industry taking off in an LEDC. These would include increased local trade, developed infrastructure, and additional industry locating in the LEDC.

3 Tourism that uses resources today without damaging the environment and people for the future.

4 Benefits include increased wealth, better infrastructure and new jobs outside traditional jobs in primary industry. Costs include debasement of local cultures and traditions, large-scale environmental damage to fragile ecosystems and many jobs are informal and temporary.

Case study: Tourism in the Costa del Sol, Spain

1 The effects are both positive and negative. Tourism has improved the infrastructure and employment levels. It has also saved local communities and traditions from dying out. Some natural landscapes have also been protected from environmental damage. However, tourism provides mainly temporary and low-paid employment. Crime has increased and traditional lifestyles have been eroded. There has been much environmental damage, with ugly high-rise buildings and traffic congestion in resorts, litter and sea pollution, as well as pressure on limited water supplies.

2 The Costa Del Sol is responding by banning any further high-rise development, making resort centres more attractive and encouraging people to explore surrounding historic towns and countryside.

Case study: Tourism in Kenya

1 Primary resources are beaches, reefs, wildlife, and a hot year-round climate.
Secondary resources are diverse cultures and good airport and road links.

2 Possible answers include: damaging fragile ecosystems (e.g. coral reefs), overuse of resources (e.g. water), frightening animals and soil erosion from safari vehicles.

3 By limiting numbers at reef and safari sites and limiting or refusing to allow any development in other coastal and inland areas

Sustainable development

1 Sustainable development involves meeting the needs of the present without compromising the ability of future generations to meet their needs.

2 In a city:
sustainable development may involve reducing waste, reducing traffic congestion and ensuring a good quality of life for all residents.

In the tourism industry: sustainable development may involve educating tourists about the area they are visiting, protecting habitats and cultures, ensuring local people receive income from tourism and monitoring/reducing the number of tourists visiting some areas.

3 Some people feel that extreme poverty, war, conflict and the global economy threaten sustainability.

Sustainable resource use

1 Renewable resources can be reused or replaced. Non-renewable resources will run out one day.

2 Your answer should look at both people and the environment. Structure your answer by dividing it into two sections. Make sure that you discuss both the advantages and disadvantages of coal mining:
People:
+ creates jobs and a strong mining community. As a mining town develops, investment and services are attracted to the area.
– When the coal supplies run low, the mine closes. This creates unemployment and services will be forced to close.

The environment:
– mining creates traffic and destroys parts of the natural landscape. It is very difficult to re-landscape an old mining area. Coal produces waste material which must be stored.

3 Humans can use resources more sustainably by reducing waste, reusing materials and recycling. Alternatives to some of the resources we use may also be found.

Resources and energy production

1 Pollution is generated which harms the environment, fossil fuels are non-renewable.

2 Acid rain is an international problem as it can be carried large distances by the wind. This means that many countries may be affected by acid rain. The country affected by acid rain may not be the country that caused the pollution.

3 Wind power does not produce waste, is non-polluting and quite cheap to set up. However, the turbines are noisy and visually intrusive so they need to be located in remote exposed areas. Many turbines are needed to generate worthwhile supplies electricity.

Managing water resources

1 Supplies are highest in Wales, Severn Trent and Thames regions and lowest in Northumbria and Southern regions. In the North and West supplies are purely surface water but in the South and East groundwater is more heavily relied upon.

2 In MEDCs the main techniques involve reducing consumption through installing water meters, introducing hosepipe bans and advertising to encourage people to waste less water. In LEDCs the main techniques involve increasing and regulating water supply through using rainwater harvesters, tube wells and by building dams.

3 Water management is harder in LEDCs as there is less capital to invest in building dams and fewer people with the expertise to develop these projects. There is often a reliance on aid to roll out large water management schemes and on charities to educate local people on how to improve their supplies.

Last-minute learner

- **These six pages give you the most important facts across the whole subject in the smallest possible space.**
- **You can use these pages as a final check.**
- **You can also use them as you revise as a way to check your learning.**
- **You can cut them out for quick and easy reference.**

Natural hazards
- The distribution of earthquakes, volcanoes and fold mountains can be explained by the theory of plate tectonics. The Earth's crust is broken up into pieces called **plates**. These plates float upon the semi-molten magma of the Earth's mantle. Huge convection currents in the mantle cause the plates to move. The point at which two plates move is called a plate boundary.
- Some plates move towards each other, some move apart and others slide past each other in opposite directions. This creates different types of plate boundaries (**constructive**, **destructive** and **conservative**).
- **Earthquakes** are caused by the sudden, violent movement of the one or two of the Earth's plates.
- The shock waves from an earthquake will be strongest nearer to its **epicentre**.
- The damage caused by an earthquake can be divided into **primary effects** (immediate impacts, such as roads and buildings collapsing) and **secondary effects** (e.g. damage to communications and fires caused by gas leaks), which can be more destructive.
- Volcanoes occur when magma from within the mantle is forced upwards to the Earth's surface.
- **Volcanoes** can be classified by their shape and type of lava (i.e. **cone** and **shield volcanoes**). They can also be classified as **active**, **dormant** or **extinct** depending on how often they erupt and when they last erupted.

- **Fold mountains** are formed when two plates collide forcing the surface rock up into mountains.
- Earthquakes and volcanic eruptions can have a great impact upon people and places. They can destroy homes and take people's lives. However, people can take steps to plan and prepare for tectonic hazards. Also there are advantages to living near volcanoes.
- **Tropical storms** are another natural hazard. Tropical cyclones and hurricanes are intense low-pressure systems that form over warm oceans (over 27 °C) usually in late summer/early autumn. They are very violent storms, with extremely strong winds and heavy rainfall.
- Like tectonic hazards, a tropical storm can have a great impact on people, the economy and the environment. Some people believe that global warming will lead to a rise in tropical storms.
- **Droughts** are a natural hazard; however, they can be made worse by human activity. Droughts are caused when there is not enough rain over an extended period of time to support people or crops. Droughts occur in semi-arid and arid areas that have experienced prolonged anticyclonic conditions.
- Humans can induce drought conditions by overusing existing water supplies and by removing trees. These activities can lead to **desertification**.

Rocks and weathering
- Rocks are classified by the way they were formed, their composition and the geological time period when they were formed.
- **Igneous rocks** (e.g. granite and basalt) were formed when magma from inside the Earth cooled and solidified.
- **Sedimentary rocks** (e.g. sandstone, chalk and limestone) formed from fragments of other rocks, or from the remains of living things being compressed into rocks.
- **Metamorphic rocks** are igneous or sedimentary rocks that have been changed through intense heat and pressure (e.g. limestone becomes marble).

- Rock type (geology) influences the shape of the landscape. Stronger rocks form highlands. The permeability of rocks determines whether the landscape is wet or dry at the surface.
- **Weathering** is the breakdown of rocks at the surface or underneath soil without any movement. **Erosion** involves movement and is the wearing away of land by water, ice or wind.
- **Physical weathering** usually results from changes in temperature or pressure. **Chemical weathering** occurs when chemicals dissolved in water attack and break down rock surfaces.

Glaciation

- **Glaciers** weather and erode the landscape by **freeze-thaw weathering**, **abrasion** and **plucking**.
- Glaciers change the shape of the landscape, widening, straightening and deepening valleys.
- When ice melts, rock material is deposited by a glacier or by meltwater streams. Glacial meltwater picks up, moves and deposits material. **Moraine** is the unsorted material carried and then deposited by a glacier. **Terminal moraine** marks the furthest point reached by a glacier.

Rivers

- The **hydrological cycle** is the movement of water from the oceans to the atmosphere, then to land and back to the oceans. Some water is stored as surface water (rivers and lakes), in groundwater, in soil moisture and after interception on leaves. Water is transferred between different stores by evaporation, transpiration, precipitation, stem flow, infiltration, surface run-off (or overland flow), percolation, throughflow and groundwater flow (below the water table).
- Rivers **erode** in four ways – abrasion (or corrasion), attrition, hydraulic action and corrosion.
- Rivers **transport** material by traction, saltation, in suspension and in solution.
- Rivers **deposit** their load when they do not have enough energy to transport it. The ability of a river to transport its load depends on its discharge.
- Most of the landforms in the upper part of a river result from erosion. The gradient of the valley is steep and friction from the bed and banks of the channel reduces the river's energy. The river mainly erodes downwards cutting a steep V-shaped valley.
- Features resulting from erosion include potholes, rapids, waterfalls and gorges.
- In the lower part of a river, the gradient becomes gentler and there is more lateral erosion. It has a wider and deeper channel, as more water is added from tributaries.
- Large amounts of silt, mud and sand are deposited where a river slows down or becomes shallower. This **alluvium** is also deposited on the floodplain on either side of a river when it floods.
- Features resulting from river deposition include flood plains, levees, meanders, ox-bow lakes and deltas.
- The amount of water flowing past a particular point in a river, over a given period of time, is called the **discharge**.
- A flood **hydrograph** shows the relationship between precipitation and the discharge of a river. The time difference between the highest rainfall and discharge is called the lag-time. There is a greater flood risk when the discharge of a river has a short lag-time and a steep rising limb.
- **Flooding** can have both positive and negative impacts on people and places. It can destroy homes and buildings and cost lives. However, it can also add alluvium to the floodplain, making it highly fertile.
- People can try to manage flooding using **hard** and **soft engineering** methods.

Coasts

- The power of **waves** increases as the strength of the winds and the distance over which the waves have built up (the fetch of the wave) increases.
- When waves break, water runs up a beach forming the **swash** and back down the beach as the **backwash**.
- **Constructive waves** are lower waves with a strong swash and weaker backwash that build up beaches. **Destructive waves** have a stronger backwash and erode material from a beach.
- Waves erode coastlines by abrasion (or corrasion), hydraulic action, attrition and corrosion.
- Material is transported along a coast by **longshore drift**.
- The type of rock and its resistance to erosion influences the way in which coastal landforms develop. Headlands form in harder rocks that are more resistant to erosion. Weaker rocks are eroded to form bays.
- **Hard engineering techniques** for protecting coastlines include the use of sea walls, gabions, rock armour and revetments. Sea walls deflect waves. Gabions, rock armour and revetments aim to dissipate or absorb the energy of waves.
- **Soft engineering techniques** aim to work with natural processes to protect coastlines. These include the rebuilding of beaches (beach nourishment) using sand dredged from further offshore. Managed retreat allows natural processes to take their course until the coast finds its own balance. Landowners near eroding coasts are moved inland and compensated for the loss of land.

Weather and climate

- **Weather** describes the daily condition of the atmosphere in a place.
- **Climate** describes the average weather conditions over a period of time.
- The world can be divided into climatic zones according to variations in temperature and the amount of precipitation.
- The temperature of a place is influenced by its latitude, distance from the sea, height above sea level, aspect and where the prevailing winds come from. Inland areas have a **continental climate** with a large range of temperatures (hot summers, colder winters). Areas near to or surrounded by the sea have a **maritime climate** with cool summers and milder winters.
- The UK has a cool, temperate (without extremes of temperature), maritime climate.
- The weather and climate of the UK is influenced by air masses – very large volumes of air of similar temperature and humidity (moisture content). The weather brought by an air mass depends on its origin and whether it passes over land or sea.
- **Depressions** are low-pressure weather systems that bring cloud, rain and wind. They form over the Atlantic where warm, tropical air meets cold, polar air and are responsible for the changeable, unsettled weather experienced by Britain over large parts of the year.
- **Anticyclones** are areas of high pressure in which air is sinking. They usually bring dry and settled weather, because sinking air warms up and can hold more moisture. Fog, mist, poor visibility and poor air quality can result from anticyclonic weather conditions.

- **Polar** and **tundra environments** are cold environments located in the far northern hemisphere and the Antarctic region. Biodiversity is low in such areas and the land is covered in snow and ice for much of the year. However, many cold environments are home to important reserves of minerals and resources (e.g. oil). This makes them attractive sites for development. Tourism is also popular in many cold environments. Antarctica is protected against development by the Antarctic Treaty.
- **Hot desert environments** are found between the Tropics of Cancer and Capricorn. They experience low rainfall and high day-time temperatures. Temperatures fall at night (due to clear skies). Like cold environments, biodiversity is low. However, resources and minerals can also be found in many hot desert areas and they are attractive for tourism. It is important to manage human activity in hot desert areas to prevent further desertification.
- The **greenhouse effect** is a natural process, which keeps the Earth warm enough for human inhabitation. However, human activity may be enhancing the greenhouse effect and causing temperatures to rise. This is called **global warming**. Global warming is controversial and not everyone agrees that it is happening.
- Some scientists suggest that this global warming may be responsible for the increasing number and strength of extreme weather and climatic events (e.g. floods, hurricanes and droughts). International agreements (e.g. The Washington Declaration) are aimed at reducing carbon emissions and reducing the impacts of global warming.

Ecosystems

- An **ecosystem** is the relationship between living (biotic) and non-living (abiotic) things.
- The different parts of an ecosystem are linked together by a series of energy and nutrient flows.
- Energy moves through an ecosystem by one member eating another in a food chain. Food webs are more complex, being made up of a series of inter-linked chains. During each stage of a food chain, energy will be lost through processes such as respiration.
- There are a number of other important cycles in ecosystems, including the **water cycle**, **carbon cycle** and **nutrient cycle**.
- A **biome** is a large-scale ecosystem.

- **Tropical rainforests** are an important ecosystem. They are found close to or on the equator and are home to many of the world's plants and animals. This great biodiversity is due to high inputs of light, heat and rain. The rainforest is structured with four layers: the emergents, the canopy, the lower canopy and the forest floor.
- Tropical rainforests are home to many important resources, particularly wood and land. Many rainforest areas are exploited for these resources. This often involves removing the trees. This disrupts the ecosystem and harms biodiversity. Many groups of people campaign for sustainable development of rainforest areas.

Population

- Populations change as a result of **births**, **deaths** and **migration**. The world's population is growing rapidly, with the most rapid growth taking place in LEDCs. Most MEDCs have slow rates of population growth with low birth rates. In some MEDCs the population is slowly declining due to very low birth rates. Most MEDCs are experiencing an ageing population.
- The **demographic transition model** shows how the population of many European countries has changed over time.
- **Population pyramids** show the numbers of males and females in different age groups in a population. The shape of a population pyramid tells a lot about the structure of a country's population.
- LEDCs have many young, dependent groups (under 15). Improving education and family planning services has helped some LEDCs to reduce birth rates.
- The number of elderly dependants in MEDCs is growing. This is due to higher life expectancy. These elderly people need to be supported with pensions, health and welfare services. Japan is an example of a country dealing with the problem of an ageing population.
- **Migration** is the movement of people from one place to another.
- **Push factors** are the negative reasons forcing or persuading people to leave an area.
- **Pull factors** are the positive reasons attracting people to a new area.
- **Rural–urban migration** is common in many LEDCs and describes the movement of people from the countryside to live in towns and cities. In MEDCs there have been more movements of people away from cities to live in rural areas (**counter-urbanisation**).
- **Refugees** are people who have been forced to leave their homes as a result of wars, political or religious conflict, or due to environmental hazards, such as floods or famine.

Urban settlement

- The level of **urbanisation** of a country or region is the proportion of its total population living in urban areas. MEDCs already have high levels of urbanisation; many LEDCs are currently urbanising rapidly.
- There are often distinctive **patterns of land use** in cities. In MEDCs the quality of housing tends to increase as you move out from the centre. In LEDCs higher quality housing is usually found just outside the CBD and poorer quality housing on the edge of the city.
- Many inner-city areas in MEDCs have been in decline since World War 2; losing both employment and population. De-industrialisation left large areas of derelict land.
- Over the last 50 years many different policies and schemes have been put in place to try to **redevelop** and **regenerate** inner-city areas.
- Many MEDC cities suffer from problems of **traffic congestion**. Various strategies have been put in place to manage this problem (e.g. traffic calming and congestion charging).

Many MEDC cities also experience socio-economic inequalities. People living in certain areas do not have access to good housing or services and they experience a poor quality of life. National governments and local councils often try to address these inequalities.

- LEDC cities are growing rapidly due to high levels of **rural–urban migration** and **high rates of natural increase** in urban areas. Many new migrants to LEDC cities find a home in squatter settlements.
- **Squatter settlements** are the unplanned settlements often built illegally at very high densities by the very poor (usually migrants from rural areas) in cities in LEDCs. They are built from cheap materials, often on poor quality land, and lack basic services.
- **Self-help** schemes (e.g. providing low-cost materials, low-interest loans to set up businesses and improve healthcare and education) and **site-and-service** schemes are positive strategies that have helped to improve the quality of life for people living in squatter settlements.

The changing countryside

- The **urban–rural fringe** is the point at which the countryside meets the city.
- In an attempt to stop urban sprawl in the UK, **green belts** were set up around several cities in the 1940s. Most types of development were not allowed within the green belts.
- **Counter-urbanisation** is a process taking place in many MEDCs with people moving from urban areas to rural areas. Counter-urbanisation can have a negative impact upon rural areas; it can alter

population structures and affect local services.

- In many rural parts of the UK, farming is still important, however farming in MEDCs has undergone great changes in recent years. Technology has developed and farming does not employ many people. Many farmers have chosen to diversify in order to continue making a profit. **Diversification** may include setting up a campsite or selling farm produce. Many farmers in MEDCs are also trying to reduce their impact upon the environment.

- Farming is still the main source of employment in many LEDCs. There are a wide variety of farming systems in LEDCs, from small subsistence farms and pastoral nomadism to large commercial plantations growing cash crops.
- Rapid population growth in many LEDCs has led to increased population pressure. Developments in farming (including the Green Revolution and new farm technology) have resulted in increases in food production. However, there is also a growing number of people who are trying new, more localised and sustainable forms of farming and rural improvement in LEDCs (e.g. the Millennium Promise Project in Malawi).

The global economy
- **Globalisation** is helping to shape the modern global economy. Globalisation involves people and places becoming more and more connected with each other. This has happened through improvements in communications and transport technology. However, not everyone benefits from globalisation and some feel that the world trade system is unfair.
- Economic activities can be classified according to the types of job people do – **primary** (extraction of raw materials and collection of food), **secondary** (manufacturing and construction), **tertiary** (services) and **quaternary** (specialist information and expertise, e.g. research and marketing).
- The employment structure of a country shows what jobs people do: in LEDCs, a high proportion work in primary industries; in MEDCs, the highest proportion work in tertiary industries and there are more quaternary activities.
- There are several important factors influencing the location of manufacturing industries – raw materials, power, markets, labour supply, transport, capital (investment), enterprise and government policy.
- **Heavy manufacturing industries** have declined in MEDCs as the raw materials have run out and can be mined more cheaply in other countries. This is called de-industrialisation and has resulted in high unemployment and environmental problems (e.g. derelict land and factories, polluted land, slag heaps).
- **High-technology industries** are common in many MEDCs. They use advanced and often expensive techniques to design and manufacture high-value technologically-sophisticated products, including consumer electronics, biotechnology, pharmaceuticals and medical equipment. They are footloose industries, usually involving the mass production and assembly of components. They often locate in clusters near to research and development facilities and sources of skilled labour (e.g. in science parks with links to universities).
- In recent years, a few very large trans-national corporations (**TNCs**) have taken control of industrial production and world trade. Transnational corporations have offices, factories and branch plants in several countries. Their headquarters are usually in MEDCs or, in some cases, in Newly Industrialising Countries (NICs).
- Many LEDC economies are developing and some are set to become NICs. However, some countries in sub-Saharan Africa may be unlikely to reach this stage of development due to problems such as war, conflict, poor infrastructure and the global trade system.

An unequal world
- The level of development of a country or region describes its wealth, level of economic growth and standards of living.
- An **MEDC** is a More Economically Developed Country.
- An **LEDC** is a Less Economically Developed Country.
- Development can be measured using economic indicators such as Gross National Product or more composite indicators such as the HDI. Social indicators can also be used (e.g. life expectancy, infant mortality, birth and death rates and adult literacy rates).
- There are eight **millennium development goals** set by the United Nations and aimed at eradicating extreme poverty by 2015.
- International trade involves buying goods and services from other countries (imports) and selling goods and services to other countries (exports). The difference between the value of imports and exports is known as the balance of trade.
- Over 80% of world trade involves MEDCs. Many LEDCs rely on exporting a narrow range of primary products. Patterns of colonial trade created a state of dependency, with LEDCs relying on MEDCs to buy their primary products and to supply them with manufactured goods. This dependency has contributed to problems of international debt.
- **Aid** is any kind of help given to a country or a group of people to improve their quality of life (money, goods, equipment and technology, expertise and training). **Emergency relief** is short-term aid to solve immediate problems. **Long-term aid** aims to bring about long-lasting improvements to quality of life.
- There are three main types of aid – **bilateral aid** (one country to another), **multilateral aid** (from several countries through organisations like the UN) and **non-government aid** (including charities).
- **Top-down development projects** are usually expensive, large-scale projects with many aims (e.g. multi-purpose dam schemes). **Bottom-up projects** include small scale self-help schemes using local materials, intermediate (appropriate) technology and involving local people. They do not rely on expensive technology brought in from outside the area. 'Bottom-up' projects are often considered more sustainable.

Tourism

- Tourism is one of the world's largest and fastest-growing industries. This growth has resulted from improvements in transport, higher incomes (in MEDCs) and more people having longer paid holidays.
- In the United Kingdom, **rural tourism** is important, with millions of people visiting **National Park** areas every year. National Parks have been established to preserve and enhance the natural beauty, wildlife and cultural heritage of areas of outstanding natural beauty.
- National Parks aim to promote enjoyment of the countryside in these areas, as well as giving attention to the social and economic needs of local communities. There can be conflicts of interest between different groups of people using the land in these National Parks.
- The growth of tourism in many LEDCs has brought economic benefits through the **multiplier effects** of investment in tourist development (e.g. employment in construction, hotels, transport, tourist amenities and services), leading to improvements in infrastructure and public services. However, tourism has also bought problems to many LEDCs. For example, fragile ecosystems can be damaged and the income from tourism often leaks back to MEDCs.
- Many LEDCs are keen to promote sustainable tourism (e.g. ecotourism). **Ecotourism** involves visiting areas with ecological resources (wildlife, environment and scenery) and human resources (traditional cultures, skills and buildings). Tourists are encouraged to learn about conserving the resources of the areas.

Sustainable development

- **Sustainable development** is development that meets the needs of the present without compromising the ability of future generations to meet their own needs.
- Sustainable development involves supporting the environment, economy and society.
- Local, national and international targets have been set to encourage sustainable development.
- Using **resources** sustainably is an important part of sustainable development. A resource is something that people can make use of. All industries rely on an input of resources. As a country develops and begins to industrialise, it uses more resources.
- Natural resources can be classified as renewable or non-renewable. **Renewable resources** will not run out (e.g. wind, sun, etc). **Non-renewable resources** are finite (e.g. coal, oil, natural gas, etc.).
- Most of the world's energy is generated using non-renewable **fossil fuels**. Burning fossil fuels can have a serious impact on the environment, including creating acid rain and contributing to global warming.
- Nuclear power is cleaner and more efficient, but there are serious safety concerns associated with it.
- Types of renewable energy include wind power, solar power, tidal power and geothermal power. All have their own advantages and disadvantages.
- Managing the Earth's water resources is an another important aspect of sustainability. In many areas supply does not match demand. Currently MEDCs use more water than LEDCs, however demand for water is rising in many LEDCs as they industrialise.
- In the UK water is managed by water authorities. In LEDCs **water management** is carried out on a more local level.